Accident, Manslaughter or Murder?

by Anthony Hunt

*QuercuS

****

QuercuS
John Roberts
67, Cliffe Way, Warwick
CV34 5JG   01926 776363

****

Accident,
Manslaughter or Murder?

by Anthony Hunt

ISBN 1 898136 20 3

First Published 2001

The Author

Anthony Hunt was born in Hednesford east of Cannock in 1943. His first school was St Joseph's Primary at Hednesford, followed by St Chad's Grammar School, Wolverhampton. Heading for a teaching career Tony spent three years at Dudley Teacher's Training College. After qualifying in 1964 he taught English and History in Staffordshire. He won a BA degree at the Open University in 1986 and took early retirement in 1994.

Tony's interests include writing, gardening and photography and he visits the elderly for his local church. Since he was a boy he has spent a lot of time on Cannock Chase, so the list of his interests includes natural history and walking. Having lived and worked all his life in South Staffordshire and next to the Chase, Tony has a special interest in the rich history of his area. He has written several articles on local topics for magazines, particularly *Best of British*, and his trawls through archive material led him to the local newspapers and murder.

All his notes and jottings left Tony with quite a collection of material, particularly 19th century murder trials and inquests. At this point he saw some QuercuS books in the shops, including the series on murders and ghosts, so he offered me the fruits of his research. The book makes quite grim reading but is full of interesting historical features and tragic but absorbing human dramas.

Thank you

To all the amiable and efficient staff at the archive libraries of Hanley, Wolverhampton and Lichfield who endured slow hours of my research while I had all the fun.

To the excellent Rob Cooper who chauffeured me uncomplaining to Wolverhampton, Stoke on Trent, Abbots Bromley, Rugeley, Stafford, Burton on Trent and nameless places all over the county whenever the whim took me.

To Andy Tew, whom I have never met, for his wonderful pen and ink sketches.

Contents

Murder

Murder is a subject that both tantalises and sickens the imagination. Like horrific car crashes, we tell ourselves that we don't want to see the gory spectacle, but as we pass we can't resist a tiny peek. You could dismiss this curiosity as simply morbid, but that doesn't explain why we all seem to share it. Could it be that in murders, car crashes and other human disasters we see that people very like us are involved? Do we sometimes recognise ourselves or imagine how we might have been there, as victim, witness, relative or detective? Do we sometimes understand the events and pressures which drove someone to kill so that we can even see ourselves in the role of murderer? Perhaps that is not really morbid, just human.

At all events, this intense interest, a feeling of being involved in murder, has been fed enthusiastically for the past couple of centuries by news reports, novels, radio plays, films and TV. Murders can be so much more satisfactory if you make them up, with all the right people murdered, and so detective story writers are an indispensable part of life. Some fictional detectives like Morse, Frost and others, have become irresistible cult figures.

As an avid reader of detective stories I began to wonder whether their bizarre storylines were ever based on actual crimes, so with the Victorian era as my starting point, I began to research books about actual murders. At first my inner detective wanted to look at unsolved crimes, but the more I saw the more I found that some officially solved murders left an uneasy feeling that somehow, the outcome was not quite right. Perhaps the sentence of the court seemed grossly unfair or I sensed a mistake in the trial.

As my appetite for such cases became more voracious I started to read Staffordshire's local newspapers. They were an historical goldmine. Happily for me, most librarians of the 18th and early 19th centuries had the foresight to realise the value of local papers as historical documents and stored them. Most large libraries now have collections of such papers on film or disc.

I can't stress too much how valuable newspapers can be to the local amateur historian, and their history is interesting in itself. I made a few notes about the papers which provided material for this book:

Wolverhampton had its *Chronicle* which started in 1789. A Saturday supplement came out in 1855 and from this grew the *Midland Counties Saturday Express*. The *Evening Star* started separately in 1880 but the two papers amalgamated in 1884 to form the *Evening Express & Star*.

1

In **Lichfield** the *Mercury* was launched in 1815 with a major report of the Battle of Waterloo. However it closed in 1833 and the modern paper grew from a revived *Mercury* started in 1877 by a Lichfield printer.

In the **Potteries** a paper with the neat title of the *Staffordshire Sentinel and Commercial and General Advertiser* was launched by a local printer as a weekly in 1854. In 1876 an offshoot called the *Daily Sentinel* came out and it is now simply called *The Sentinel*.

Stafford had another venerable newspaper, the *Staffordshire Advertiser* launched in 1795. In a sense it continues in the shape of the *Stafford Chronicle* which took over the *Advertiser* in 1972.

Up to the 1880s very few people could read and these newspapers published weekly editions. However, several events changed the whole basis of newspaper readership and circulation.

The Education Act 1870 made schooling compulsory and meant that much greater numbers of people would learn to read, and in the same year a tax on newspapers was lifted. A third factor was the invention of high speed rotary presses which made printing much cheaper. For example, the *Lichfield Mercury* was originally a massive 7d [7 old pence, a little more than 2.5p] but became 1d. The *Staffordshire Sentinel* fell from 3d to 1d while Wolverhampton's *Express and Star* was priced at half of 1d.

Newspapers were such a success that in Staffordshire most large and many small towns, like Rugeley and Hednesford, had their own titles. For the historian a wealth of new history, economic, political and social, was daily investigated, reported, distributed and then stored. In some ways this made newspapers a more fruitful source for research than others and this is why I used them for examining old murders rather than search through the original trial transcripts. It is also true that to make use of the court records you first have to have to know something about the crime you want to research, which I rarely did. I came upon most episodes in this book quite by chance, surely a fillip for any local historian.

A word of warning though, when using newspapers as historical sources, reporters very soon learnt how to manipulate their readers. Although factual evidence is rarely incorrect, interpretation of the facts can vary according to what the reporter thought his readers might want to see. For example, in the story *Beer and Ice Cream* the reports took a rabidly racist line against Italians until the editor realised that the people of Wolverhampton were alarmed. Suddenly the reports changed tack. Perhaps the trial judge also had something to say about interfering with the course of justice, though that would not have been reported.

We have featured some of the headlines used by the various newspapers as illustrations. However, the originals did not reproduce well and so what you see are modern reconstructions using similar typefaces.

Courts, Juries and Penalties

Victorian legal procedures were in some ways similar to those of today. If the police wanted to hold a suspect, then as now, they had to take them before the local Magistrates' Courts. This was (and is) sometimes known as the Stipendiary Court when the bench consists of just one professional magistrate instead of the usual three lay people. Today there is a 36 hour limit to holding a suspect. Victorian magistrates invariably allowed a week or longer before the police had to return to ask for more time.

Once the police felt they had enough evidence they needed to bring the suspect to trial. Minor crimes could be heard in the Magistrates' Court, but there are no minor murders so, with other serious offences, they were tried before a judge and jury. Our main criminal court is now the Crown Court, but until quite recently this type of trial was conducted in Assizes or Quarter Sessions. Assizes sat in county towns, in this case Stafford, to hear cases arising anywhere in Staffordshire except the boroughs. Quarter Sessions were the equivalent courts for the larger towns which had attained the self governing status of boroughs, such as Hanley, Wolverhampton and Walsall, but they sat only four times a year. However, very serious cases, and especially those which might involved the death penalty, were always heard by the most senior and experienced judges, so murder cases in Staffordshire always went to the Assize Court at Stafford.

For people found guilty of murder or manslaughter there were three types of sentence. Until 1957 the penalty for murder was death. If the jury decided that the case did not amount to murder because the accused did not intend to kill (or cause serious harm), they should have brought a verdict of manslaughter. For this offence the penalty was, and still is, at the discretion of the judge within a statutory limit of imprisonment for life. He might simply imprison the guilty person for whatever period he thought suitable, or in the past he could impose a period of penal servitude.

This was introduced in 1853 as an alternative to transportation because the people of the new Australia were begining to ask why they had to go on being a dumping ground for British convicts. Broadly, it was goal with forced labour in which different proportions of imprisonment and work could be set by the judge. So convicts might be sent to quarries breaking rocks for roadstone or set to excavating harbours.

Before a person could be tried at the Assizes or Quarter Sessions, as with the Crown Court today, they had to be committed for trial in the Magistrates' Court. The magistrates are not trying the case but carrying out a sifting function. They hear the case for the prosecution and as much from the defence as that side want to say at this stage, and from this decide whether there is enough evidence to form a case for the accused to answer. The aim is to weed out hopeless and unjustified prosecutions and to tell the accused what he is charged with so that he can prepare a defence.

There used to be another route by which a person could be committed, which was by a Coroner's jury. The Coroner has existed since at least 1194 and, as the name suggests, he is an officer of the crown. They have performed various functions over the centuries, but by the 19th century they had two: a minor duty to decide whether buried treasure was Treasure Trove and their main job of investigating unnatural or violent deaths.

The Coroner had and still has to establish the identity of the dead person and determine how, when and where they died. In Victorian times he must summon a jury of 12 men, changed by an Act of 1887 to a group of between 7 and 11, and could call whatever witnesses he thought might be helpful. The procedure remains quite unlike any other court in the United Kingdom because it is inquisitorial. In other words, there are no sides, prosecution and defence, to present a case and call witnesses, it is an inquisition or investigation by the coroner. Both the Coroner and the jury could question witnesses, and the jury often did so. Interested parties such as relations of the deceased or someone accused of causing the death, might be represented and put questions to witnesses at the Coroner's discretion. The accused need only appear before this court if they wished to and they could only be cross examined with their agreement.

After the evidence had been heard the Coroner would sum up the evidence and ask the jury to bring a verdict, which might be an open verdict or that the deceased had died as a result of accident, suicide, murder or manslaughter. If they named the person they thought was responsible that acted as an indictment and the coroner could commit them for trial. Today most cases are heard without a jury and although Coroners may still say that death was caused unlawfully, they must not name anyone.

Equally, the Coroner's jury might decide that the accused had no case to answer. This they almost did in the case of William Narrowmore in the story, *Victoria Intervenes*. The jury felt that he should not have to stand trial, but the coroner knew the wishes of the police and magistrates and committed him to be tried at Stafford Assizes.

Narrowmore's case underlines the fact that all trials are likely to show large or small differences of opinion over the meaning of facts. Our legal system depends largely on human beings and their opinions, which is both its greatest strength and its greatest weakness. Reading these cases you may feel, as I did, that some of the decisions of the courts were suspect, or at least, very strange. However, until we can devise a better system they will go on answering the tantalising question in murder cases – Was it Accident, Manslaughter or Murder?

The grimly traditional old courtroom in Hanley Town Hall is no longer in use but Quarter Sessions were held here from 1880. The most serious cases, including murder trials, would have been heard at Stafford Assizes.

Dead and Ditched
(Alrewas 1885 - Lichfield Mercury)

What would you do if getting the price of even the most meagre next meal seemed impossible. And what if you had your little child to feed? Theft would seem to be the answer, but would you contemplate murder? Not the killing of a stranger that you might rob, but of your child to end its misery. Is that what Elizabeth Riley did on 9th May 1885?

No one ever discovered what desperation drove Elizabeth Riley and her eight year old Mary to be wandering the country lanes between Lichfield and Burton on Saturday 9th May. Several people had seen the couple but had taken little notice. Both mother and child were quite reasonably dressed and did not seem distressed. Later that day some of the same people saw Elizabeth alone, but again saw nothing to worry them.

On the following morning three or four young boys were out collecting flowers near Hillyard's Cross when they came upon the body of a child in the ditch by West Hill Road. She seemed quite peaceful and at first the boys were not sure whether she was dead or just asleep. They decided to find an adult and the first person they saw was John Swingler who was crossing the common between Streethay and Fradley to visit a farmer friend. The group of excited lads persuaded him to come with them to the ditch and realising that the little girl was dead, he sent the lads off to find other help.

Two local farmers, Mr Giles and Mr Pegg, arrived at the scene and it was Mr Pegg who went for the police. When Constable Martin arrived he had the body taken to the Bull's Head Inn. It was not long before news of the awful find spread round the villages and soon Sergeant Harrison of Alrewas Station, then in charge of the first investigation, had enough information to issue a description of the child's mother.

Because the crime involved the death of a young child local people were glad to help the police, and many sightings of Elizabeth Riley were recorded. She had been seen in Lichfield on the evening of Saturday 9th May and later that night in the Holly Bush public house. From there she had gone back to Birmingham where she had found a bed for the Sunday night at the Union Workhouse.

It was at the workhouse that Superintendent Gilbridge found Elizabeth Riley and asked her to come with him back to Alrewas. At the Coroner's inquest he reported that Elizabeth was in a most distressed condition as they travelled back to the crime scene. She had told him, "I should have given myself up tomorrow if you had not come when I had seen the local papers". She had nearly fainted several times as they had waited at New Street Station for the 5.20 pm train to Alrewas. The Superintendent said that throughout the journey she seemed deeply regretful for what she had done.

But what had she done? All the circumstances pointed to murder, but there were several anomalies. Why was the corpse so respectfully laid to rest that the arms had been neatly folded across the bosom, and why were there no external marks of violence? But if the child had died of natural causes, why had Elizabeth Riley simply walked away from her daughter's body and never tried to inform anyone.

Her contradictory actions might suggest either love or callousness. So was it murder or just some terrible twist of fate that left poor Mary Riley in a makeshift grave in a quiet country lane?

MYSTERIOUS OCCURENCE NEAR LICHFIELD.

THE DEAD BODY OF A CHILD FOUND IN A DITCH.

A modern copy of the Mercury's headline.

When the inquest opened at the Bull's Head Inn on Tuesday 12th May, Mr Morgan, the Coroner, concluded that the child had died in very suspicious circumstances, either from suffocation or congestion of the lungs brought on by an acute cold. The true cause of death would not be fully known until a post mortem could be held and so he adjourned the hearing until the following week.

Elizabeth Riley appeared before the Coroner that day, but she was in such a wretched state, crying all through the hearing, that they learnt little from her. She admitted that she had lost her husband six years previously and had since lived as a pauper. She did have relatives in Pelsall but did not wish them to know about her circumstances. Unable to gain anything more from her, the Coroner handed her over to the police who took her to Tamworth Police Station. The following day she was charged with the murder of her daughter.

When the inquest resumed on Monday 18th May everything seemed set for Mr Morgan to discover what had really happened to young Mary Riley, but things did not go to plan.

John Swingler described how he had come upon the corpse, insisting that he just lifted the body from the ditch and placed it on the bank exactly as it had lain in the ditch. On no account had he folded the arms over the chest. It was their position that had fooled the boys at first. Swingler remembered one lad saying, "Here's a little girl asleep", because she looked so peaceful.

The next witness was Mary Ann Usher who had been taking her husband's tea to him when she spotted a woman and child on the Burton Road. Later on she came across the woman again, but that time she was alone. The woman was heading towards the Trent Valley Hotel where she took shelter for a while. Though not together, the pair of them had walked along the road to Lichfield. As they reached the town, the woman headed off in a different direction.

When questioned, Mary Usher was quite clear that the woman had appeared perfectly normal, though she thought it strange that the child was missing. She would never have suspected that some mischief had been done because the prisoner seemed in no way alarmed.

So far both witnesses had said that they would have been amazed if a murder had been committed, but the Coroner needed more evidence to establish the cause of death. He hoped that this would be provided by Mr Rogers, the surgeon.

From the beginning of his evidence Mr Rogers made it disarmingly clear that he had little experience in performing post mortems. In fact, he had to admit that that was his first without assistance from an experienced surgeon. He had concluded that the child had died from congestion of the lungs, but how that had occurred he could not say. He confessed that the only reason for arriving at that decision was the lack of external injuries.

Mr Morgan asked for a second post mortem. This time Mr Lowe, a highly experienced surgeon from Burton on Trent, would help Mr Rogers. The surgeons were asked to perform the post mortem that evening and report their findings the following day.

By the following morning, Tuesday 19th, the second post mortem had been completed and Mr Lowe suggested that death would not have been caused by congestion because that was usually accompanied by other signs, and there were none. He thought it more likely that the cause of death was asphyxia or paralysis of the nervous system brought about by some violent shock. One possible cause of that paralysis might possibly be a fit, but he would not say that such an event had definitely occurred.

The inquest was therefore offered the uncertain possibility of suffocation as the cause of death. But that was difficult to relate to Elizabeth Riley's calm behaviour after the crime, if one occurred, unless she was quite the most callous person they had ever encountered. Her pathetic demeanour in previous hearings would suggest otherwise, as would the evidence of two further witnesses.

Robert Swingler, no relation to John Swingler, had been driving a baker's cart on the afternoon of 9th May when he came across Elizabeth and little Mary sitting on a bridge near Wychnor. Returning along the same road at about 5.30 pm, he saw the woman sitting alone under the hedge, her feet dangling over the ditch where the body would later be found. He had spoken to the woman but she would have nothing to do with him. She seemed scared that he might do her harm and to ward him off said that her husband was not far off and would be along soon. Not wanting to alarm her he had left.

In his description of the woman and child, Robert Swingler said that the pair were not "like common tramps". The child was dressed in a black dress, trimmed with velvet. She had a fur tippet (shoulder cape) and a broad brimmed straw hat, also trimmed with velvet, and a peacock feather. She wore good button shoes and dark clothing, which was neat and respectable. It was their appearance that led Robert to believe that there was nothing wrong. Mother and daughter seemed quite happy together, as did Elizabeth when he saw her alone.

Annie Beach, a servant of Mr Royals of Fradley Common, was the final witness. One of her duties was to take the cows from the fields to the farm, and while she was doing that she had seen the woman and child sitting on the grass verge. Later she had seen the woman alone. Annie told the court that the child had seemed well at the time and had been talking in a pleasant voice. Nothing in the behaviour of mother or child had suggested that anything was amiss.

On one hand the witnesses who saw Elizabeth Riley suggested that she had seemed perfectly normal and relaxed, before and after the tragedy, hardly the actions of a murderess. On the other hand her statement to Sergeant Gilbridge that she would have turned herself in to the police and, rather weakly, the medical evidence, suggested foul play.

The report of the case in the *Lichfield Mercury* mentions only the Coroner and not the jury, which there must have been, nor does it mention their verdict. However, it must have been one of unlawful killing because they decided there was enough evidence to commit Elizabeth Riley for trial at Stafford Assizes.

When the trial opened on Thursday 30th July 1885 the prosecution produced no further evidence. The two police surgeons were still unsure of the exact cause of Mary's death. In fact, having had time to reflect on the post mortems, they were even less decided. They agreed that she could have died from a fit, but would not swear to it; or she could have been suffocated, and they would not swear to that either.

As their evidence was the only possible way of deciding whether Mary's death was an accident or murder, Mr Justice Smith had to direct the jury to acquit, and so Elizabeth Riley walked free.

What really happened to Mary Riley is still a mystery. If she died in her mother's arms and not at her mother's hands, then Elizabeth Riley had suffered another terrible blow in her miserable life. Yet why would such a caring mother just walk away from her daughter's corpse. Perhaps in her destitute state she thought the cost of a funeral was impossible to bear and so did the only thing she could. The ditch became the simple grave and the body laid to rest as peacefully and respectfully as Elizabeth knew how.

Ladies of the Fradley area were so alarmed and disturbed by the sad story that they organised a service, burying the body of Mary Riley at Fradley Church on 21st May 1885. We don't know whether Elizabeth ever visited the grave, but villagers tended it regularly.

Fradley Church

A Family Fight
(Burslem 1884 – Staffs Sentinel)

Thomas Scott-Garner was an unmarried potter living in Howard Street, Burslem. His younger brother, twenty-seven year old Albert, was an engine tender of nearby Haywood Street. Between 6 and 7 pm on Saturday 23rd May 1884 they were drinking together in Smith's Vaults in Haywood Street.

It seems the two had always got on well together, so perhaps alcohol was the cause of the trouble. For whatever reason, a quarrel broke out between the brothers over their respective occupations. Harmless at first, each brother gibing at the other, the mood suddenly changed and the argument became heated. Without warning, Albert swung at his brother and hit Thomas on the jaw.

From here the drunken dispute passed through an attack in an alley with attempted stangulation to a head butting incident, and Albert's death shortly after 8 o'clock the following morning. Thomas was arrested and charged with causing the death of his younger brother.

Unable to understand just why his brother had died, Thomas pleaded with the police to be allowed to sit in on the inquest. Inspector German obtained permission from the Coroner, Mr J Booth, and still in shock, Thomas was seated before the jury in the Leopard Hotel, Burslem on Monday 25th May to hear the evidence.

The first witness was Richard Foster, Thomas's neighbour and fellow worker. He stated that on the fatal Saturday evening at about 6.30 he entered Smith's Vaults and saw the two brothers drinking together. They seemed to be having an argument about engine valves, but nothing so as to make Foster worry. Suddenly though, after about ten minutes, Albert struck Thomas on the jaw. Thomas got up as if to hit Albert back, but the landlord intervened quickly and turned Albert out of the pub. Albert left by the front door and Foster followed. Outside, Albert refused to go home, but instead shouted that he would wait and "give it to his brother before he went home".

Unable to convince Albert to leave, Foster went back into the vaults and told Thomas, "if I were you, I would have no bother, but go home". Thomas agreed and Foster persuaded the landlord to let Thomas out the back way. He stayed in the vaults for another ten minutes until he was told that Albert had followed his brother home. Arriving at his own house Foster found that

Albert had caught up with his brother in the entry next to Foster's house, he had Thomas by the throat and Thomas was "quite black in the face".

Risking his own safety Foster managed to pull Albert off, telling him that he "would not have that sort of conduct in his entry". Albert's reply was that he would give it to the witness as well if he interfered again. Foster then took Thomas into his own home and tried to keep him there, but the prisoner was "excited" and determined to go out again. Eventually Foster had to let him go despite Thomas bleeding from a head wound caused when Albert had bitten him on the cheek.

Thomas immediately crossed the road after his brother and Albert saw him coming. The two ran at each other, heads down like rams. When they met there was a cracking sound and both men fell without striking any more blows. Thomas tried several times to get up and when he eventually succeeded, the witness took him into his home. Albert was still lying in the road on his back and Foster did not know how he got to his home about sixty yards away, or who took him.

That part of the story was cleared up when Albert's wife, Emily Scott-Garner, gave her evidence. She had seen her husband and his brother in Mr Foster's entry between 6 and 7 o'clock. Albert had hold of Thomas's scarf which was around Thomas's neck, and was strangling him with it. With some difficulty, she and Mr Foster managed to free Thomas and she persuaded Albert to go home with her.

A.TEW

About five minutes later, when they had gone barely a few yards, Albert saw Thomas coming after them. Both men then bent their heads and charged at one another. When their heads collided both men fell, collapsing in different directions. Albert was "quite senseless" and so she and a man named James Amos picked him up and managed to get him home.

Once in the house they put him on the sofa, but after five minutes Albert got up and vomited beer. She noticed a large lump on the left side of his head, but after bathing with a wet cloth it went down. Thinking he was just the worse for ale she then left the house and went shopping. On her return, he was in the back premises [probably outhouse toilet] and able to walk a little.

That night Albert stayed on the sofa and Emily stayed with him. At 2 o'clock she tried to wake him but couldn't. However, because he had never complained of his injury and Emily felt certain he was still quite drunk, she left him alone. It was only when he began to turn a strange colour that she realised that something was wrong and called in the doctors. Unfortunately it was too late and Albert died soon after they arrived.

When questioned by the jury Emily said that the two brothers always seemed the best of friends and had never fought before. Even during their struggle she never witnessed an actual blow, just that fatal head butt. When asked why the blow might have caused more harm to her husband than his brother, Emily said that she had no idea, but Albert had been involved in two accidents earlier in his life. About eight years ago, he had been pulled over a pulley at the colliery and had hurt himself, and two years ago he had been struck by lightening.

Whether those incidents had any bearing on the state of Albert's health was not clear and the Coroner adjourned the hearing for a post mortem. On Friday 29th May the Inquest sat again to hear the medical evidence and statements from several other witnesses.

Robert Smith, landlord of the Liverpool Arms, nicknamed Smith's Vaults, corroborated Richard Foster's evidence, as did Samuel Woodhouse, a plasterer who witnessed the argument in the pub. But it was the evidence of Doctors Oldham and Taylor that the Coroner wanted to hear. Both had been at Albert's death and had then carried out the post mortem.

They agreed that the body had no external marks of violence, but on removing the scalp they had found blood covering an area of four square inches. Further examination inside the skull revealed a blood clot which was the result of a ruptured artery. The skull itself was not fractured. In their opinion the cause of death was congestion in the skull due to the amount of blood present. The violent blow suffered in the head butting would have added add to the compression on the brain.

As to why Albert suffered a fatal blow yet Thomas did not, the doctors put it down to ill fortune. It was possible that Albert's' previous injuries may have weakened his skull, though that could not be proved. What was clear was that the clash of heads had caused the blood clot and the compression on the brain.

It was that evidence which led the Coroner's jury to hold Thomas Scott-Garner responsible for his brother's death and they returned an verdict of manslaughter, but added in the rider that he had acted under "great provocation". Nevertheless, a stunned Thomas was committed to stand trial at the next Assizes, accused of killing his brother.

FRATRICIDE AT BURSLEM.	*None of the newspaper headlines were exactly sensational, but the Sentinel was more restrained than most.*
SHOCKING RESULT OF A QUARREL.	

On 29th July 1884 a jury at the Stafford Assizes heard the evidence. The presiding judge was Baron Huddleston, who instructed them on the law. If the jury found that the two brothers had decided to attack each other, then Thomas would be guilty of manslaughter, that is, causing Albert's death while carrying out an illegal act though not intending to kill.

The jury decided that Thomas had merely tried to defend himself from an over aggressive brother. Any blame lay clearly with Albert. Thomas was acquitted, the jury adding that he would be punished enough in the knowledge that he had accidentally killed his brother.

[**Why was the judge a Baron?** In the mediaeval period when English law developed there was a Court of Exchequer in which the judges were called Barons. Originally it handled tax cases, but long before the 19th century had become one of three courts which all did similar jobs. The others were Common Pleas and Kings Bench. Reforms at the end of that century put an end to this muddle and duplication. Between 1883 and 1885 Acts of Parliament merged these courts into a single system, much as it is today. Exchequer was abolished after the retirement of its last Baron, so Baron Huddleston was a mediaeval hangover.]

The Heat of the Moment
(Burslem 1895 – Staffs Sentinel)

In any cookery book for family strife and bitterness, the main ingredients of most receipes would have to be alcohol and money. So many disputes are caused by too much of the first and a lack of the second. This was certainly what led to the horrific death of John Maitland at Burslem in 1895.

Maitland was an unemployed labourer who had lived with his "wife", Elizabeth Lowndes, at Stych Place, Burslem for some years. It was a troubled relationship. Elizabeth worked full time as a potter but often had to hand over money to her partner for alchohol. That caused many arguments, especially when John Maitland had been drinking. So frequent were their rows that the neighbours hardly bothered to complain, but even the resigned neighbours were alarmed by the fight on the night of Saturday May 25th.

Both Elizabeth and John arrived home quite drunk at around 9.30 pm. What happened in the next few hours ended with John Maitland being rushed to a local hospital with terrible burns.

Having questioned Lowndes and received rather unsatisfactory answers, Constable Peale decided to take her to the hospital where he would be able to see Maitland. Though severely burned, Maitland managed to tell the constable that his wife had thrown the lamp at him and deliberately set him on fire. Elizabeth Lowndes was arrested and charged with causing injury to her husband, but that changed to murder when Maitland died later that day.

SERIOUS OUTRAGE AT BURSLEM. A MAN SHOCKINGLY BURNED. FATAL RESULT.	*Teacher's could give their classes an amusing exercise by asking them to translate the old headline into modern terms, or vice versa.*

The inquest opened at the Leopard Hotel on 5th June 1895. Despite advice from the Coroner, Mr Booth, Elizabeth Lowndes refused any help from lawyers, preferring to represent herself.

The first witness was Constable Peale. He told the court that when he had visited the hospital, John Maitland had made a statement. He had said that Lowndes and he had been arguing over money that he was hiding in the bedroom. She had become violent and said she would cut off his hand.

Then she had thrown the lamp at him and it hit him and set his shirt on fire. He pleaded with her and she threw some water over him, but it did not put out the fire. He had raced downstairs and had torn off his shirt.

At that point in the constable's evidence, Lowndes shouted, "It's a lie. If he was alive, he ought to suffer for telling you that lie", to which Constable Peale replied that Maitland had made his statement in front of two police officers, Mrs Lovatt and her daughter.

Ignoring the Coroner's pleas for order, Lowndes went on, "He did say so, but it is a lie. We had been falling out all night and shortly before it happened he had been beating me in the yard and in the house. The row was over him taking my money off me which he was hiding when the lamp burst in his hand."

Once the courtroom had quietened down the constable continued his evidence. He said that he had gone to Stych Place and recovered the broken lamp and fragments of burnt cloth. The glass pieces had been gathered from the floor, but the lampshade was in its place and completely unbroken.

The second witness was Dr S King who had examined Maitland in hospital. He told the Court that the burns were chiefly on Maitland's back and that he had died from shock caused by their severity. He was present when Maitland gave his statement to the police and was certain that the deceased was of sound mind at the time.

When it was the turn of the Lovatts, mother and daughter, to give their evidence, they both said that they had heard Maitland's statement, but that they had also heard Elizabeth Lowndes tell them another version of the story, and they did not know who to believe. The Coroner quickly dismissed them as possible biased witnesses and called Ellen Rigby.

Ellen Rigby lived in Stych Place, directly opposite the Maitland house. She stated that on the Saturday night she had been in bed, but was awakened by a woman using bad language and accusing her partner of being with other women. Unable to get back to sleep, she had gone downstairs, opened the window and sat on the sill to hear more clearly.

During all the argument she never heard the man speak, but she did see the paraffin lamp swing back and forth three times. She saw it hit the wall, followed by the sound of breaking glass and the screams of a man. Then she heard the man shout, "Oh Lizzie, don't put no more on me, you have burnt me to death". He had screamed fearfully and flames came through the window.

Ellen Rigby added that Lowndes was mocking Maitland as he was burning until he shouted for the neighbours to help. Then Lowndes burst into tears and said, "You shouldn't have made me do it."

Questioned by the Coroner, Ellen Rigby said that she had heard everything distinctly because her window was open. When asked why she had refused to help Elizabeth Lowndes when she had come to her house for help, Rigby said that she "was afraid of her as she looked so wild".

With Ellen Rigby's evidence complete, the Coroner reviewed the evidence and the jury retired. After only five minutes they returned an indictment of Lowndes for manslaughter.

On Thursday 25th July 1895 Elizabeth Lowndes appeared at Stafford Crown Court before Mr Justice Hawkins. Once again she refused all offers of representation. Was she hoping that this might persuade the jury that she must be innocent? Only the guilty need defending?

Ellen Rigby repeated her damning evidence, adding that John Maitland had called out for his brother, Joe, who lived next door. She also added that when Lowndes had arrived at her house she asked Rigby to stay with Maitland while she ran to the hospital, not the doctor. Being afraid of the prisoner Rigby had told Lowndes to fetch another neighbour, named Lovatt.

When Elizabeth Lowndes cross examined Rigby she accused her of lying to the Court. She told the court that she had "never spoken to Rigby in her life before" until the trial. Rigby denied that.

When Julia Lovatt gave evidence she said she lived in Stych Place and in the early hours of that Sunday morning, Elizabeth Lowndes had come to her house asking for help with her husband, who had been badly burned. The prisoner had told her that she and Maitland had been arguing over money and a lamp had exploded.

She had gone to the Maitland home and found the deceased in the bedroom, lying on the bed. When she asked him what had happened, he had said, in the prisoner's presence, "You **** cat, you have done this." Realising that what he had said was dreadful, Lovatt had said, "Don't say that. It is a very serious thing if you are not certain". Maitland repeated his claim and Elizabeth Lowndes denied it.

When questioned by the prisoner, Mrs Lovatt said that the deceased had a shirt on which Lowndes had put over him as soon as she had put out the flames.

Martha Lovatt, Julia's daughter, confirmed all her mother's evidence, adding that the prisoner had told her that the lamp had exploded in "her" hand. Puzzled, the judge pointed out that in her deposition Martha had stated "his" hand. Somewhat nervous and confused by the court proceedings, Martha could only mumble that she thought Lowndes had said "her" hand, though she could be mistaken.

Who then, was telling the truth about the fatal events of Saturday, 25th May?

The court then heard Maitland's statement as taken down by Constable Peale.

"About half past ten on the 25th of May, I went to bed. Between an hour and an hour and a half later my wife, Elizabeth Lowndes, came to bed. About two o'clock in the morning I got out of bed and my wife said "You b***** thing, you are drunk". There was a lamp burning on a box near the bed and my wife threw it at me. It struck me behind the back of the neck. I had a shirt on and a cotton singlet and they set on fire and burned. I ran downstairs and tore the shirt away as well as I could. My wife said a two shilling piece I was hiding was hers, and I said it was mine. My wife tried to put the fire out by throwing some water over me and also some soap suds. I was sober. I had a pint of ale at home which I drank."

Constable Peale was the next witness. He said that it was given in the presence of Elizabeth Lowndes but as soon as she heard it she had accused Maitland of lying. Maitland responded, "I did not have a drink in the town. How could I throw the lamp at myself?" She had replied that he was drunk on that night.

Constable Peale went on to tell the court that he had been on duty when Elizabeth Lowndes arrived at the Police Station on the Sunday. In her statement she said that she had gone to bed first to get out of her husband's way. He had come upstairs directly and taken a lamp off the box to look for some money. The lamp had exploded in his hand and burned him.

It was Peale who had escorted Lowndes to the hospital, and in her presence Maitland had accused her of throwing the lamp. Because of the seriousness of the claim, the constable had told the deceased "to be careful" and had said, "Now, Jack, did she throw the lamp at you?", to which he said that she had.

Constable Shorthouse had gone with Peale to the hospital and corroborated the evidence, adding that he had asked Lowndes if any of her clothing had been burned in the fire. She said that her nightdress had been burned on the left side, but was unable to produce it.

The case for the prosecution over, Elizabeth Lowndes was asked for her defence. She produced a written statement which she read to the court. It was three years since she had first met John Maitland. They had lived together very comfortably when he was not drunk. She had left him several times when he had beaten her, but he had fetched her back. They had both worked up to two years ago, but he had had no regular work since.

On May 25th they had been to the town together and Maitland had called in several pubs while she did the shopping. When they got back to the house

he said that he had lost his key, but before she could give it to him, he had knocked her down in the entry. In the house he had hit her several times more because she would not fetch him some beer. He began to quarrel and she had to give him some money.

Soon afterwards he went to bed and she left him with some beer in a jug and a lamp on the table. When she saw him again after they had been asleep some time, he was taking money out of her skirt pocket. He had hidden it in the grate, but when he realised that she had seen him, he picked up the lamp and said that he would hide it in another place.

She had gone to get the money off him, but he had hit her in the mouth, knocking a tooth out. She had tried to hit him back but hit the lamp instead. The barrel (paraffin reservoir) cracked and the globe fell off onto her stocking. She threw water on it and tried to douse the flames.

Finally, she told the court that she was very sorry for what had happened and if the court were merciful, she would try to be a "different woman".

In an attempt to clarify what violence Maitland may have used, the judge recalled Constable Shorthouse concerning the tooth. In reply to the judge's question, the constable said that it was the first time that he had heard of a tooth being knocked out. The prisoner had not mentioned it in any of her statements.

Satisfied with the constable's statement, Mr Justice Hawkins began his summing up. He told the jury that there were three differing versions of what had taken place in the bedroom on that fatal evening.

First, John Maitland had testified that his wife threw the lamp at him; secondly, Elizabeth Lowndes said that the lamp had burst into flames while her husband was carrying it; and third, she had later altered that account to having accidentally hit the lamp whilst trying to hit out at her husband, and it had burst into flames. It was for the jury to decide which version they believed.

Further to that, he had to tell the jury that in his mind, if there had been some sort of struggle in the bedroom, then he would have expected that both participants would have had burnt clothing. Elizabeth Lowndes had none. The doctor had confirmed that the burns were on Maitland's back which supported Maitland's version. But, the judge stressed, there were no witnesses to the actual event, save for the participants.

In Lowndes' defence he did point out that she had tried to extinguish the flames and tried to get help. The jury should also remember that she had suffered provocation in the form of physical violence.

Strangely, the jury said that they had no need to retire. They unanimously found Elizabeth Lowndes guilty of throwing the lamp at her husband in a fit of passion whilst under the greatest provocation and delivered a verdict of manslaughter.

Before he passed sentence Mr Justice Hawkins told the court that if Elizabeth Lowndes had committed the crime in cold blood he would have given her a much harsher sentence, but like the jury, he was sure that she had acted in desperation. Her anger had lasted only a short time before she tried to help John Maitland. He had made the punishment as light as he could consistent with his duty to the public, and Elizabeth Lowndes was sentenced to twelve months hard labour.

If Animals Could Talk
(Burton on Trent 1828 – Staffordshire Advertiser)

What if the only eyewitness to a possible crime is an animal, and the police can only guess at what happened? This was what hampered investigations into the death of Thomas Hollier on 13th March 1828. It saw the men accused of his murder lingering in gaol for two years until the trial began at Stafford Assizes under Mr Justice Bosanquet.

An outline of events soon emerged from the evidence of several witnesses. It seems that the evening of 13th March began pleasantly enough with Hollier indulging in his favourite pastime of drinking at a regular haunt, the New Inn at Burton on Trent. He sat at one of the tables with young Thomas Batkin, son of the landlord. Hollier had a small dog on his lap which became the centre of conversation. Whether the animal was a gift for Batkin or the subject of some bet never became clear, but suddenly the young man decided to snatch the dog from its owner.

Hollier resisted and the two men started fighting. For about five minutes the struggle continued, and it ended with the two rolling around on the bar floor. Finally William Dodson, another regular customer, stepped in to stop the fight. Holding Hollier back, Dodson tried to persuade him to leave the inn. But Hollier would have none of it and he even persuaded the landlord to allow his son to continue the fight outside in the yard.

Thinking it would be over in minutes and having no doubts that his son would win, Batkin senior ushered them into the yard. As they were leaving the inn young Batkin's pal, Frederick Shorthouse, offered to second his friend by holding his coat. It all seemed rather gentlemanly.

What exactly happened in the yard is not clear, but Hollier must have lost the battle because the dog was given to Batkin. Although probably quite hurt, Hollier announced to everyone that he was not injured one bit and about an hour later, mounted his horse and rode away. As Hollier left the inn James Patrick arrived for a drink and saw him and then Batkin. He later said it had been obvious that the two men had been quarrelling.

What followed the events at the inn is where the mystery lies. William Haines, a wagoner to Mr Mason of Burton, was driving his wagon towards Four Lanes Ends when he spotted a horse grazing on the roadside. He stopped to take a closer look because the animal was all tacked up for riding, but there was no sign of a rider. He managed to catch the horse and tie it to his wagon before driving on towards the town. Not much further along the road he came across a man lying in the road, seemingly asleep. Haines had to shake him hard before he could wake him.

Assuming the man was the worse for drink Haines helped him to his feet with difficulty. He had had to grip the man tightly by the thicker part of the arm and steady him before he could help him walk across the road to recover his hat. As they walked Hollier said that his head hurt and asked Haines to examine his eye because he was sure that it must be black.

Still worried about the man, who was very groggy, Haines offered to guide him back to Burton. Hollier agreed and remounted his horse, but after riding a little of the way with Haines, Hollier said that he would go to Roadside and stay the night there with relations. Having assured Haines that he was fine, Hollier said goodnight and rode away. Whether he was truly well Haines was not sure, but about half an hour later he saw Hollier again, still riding his horse. At this second meeting Haines was convinced that Hollier had improved and seemed sober.

What had happened to Hollier in that half hour became clear from the evidence of Mary Hawthorne, a relative of Hollier. She told the court that he had turned up at her home at about 8 o'clock that evening wanting to see her husband. He had seemed distressed and asked for a candle so that her husband could inspect his eye to see whether it had turned black. When it could not be ascertained if there was a bruise, Hollier had simply thanked them and left the house to return home.

Apart from Haines catching a glimpse of him and possible attackers, no witness saw Hollier alive again.

At 5 o'clock the following morning, 14th March, a sawyer called Charles Merry was on his way to work with his son, also named Charles. As they walked up the lane called Lichfield Lane or Derby Lane (depending where you were in the lane), they came across a body lying face down with the left arm beneath it and the right arm stretched out.

Some distance away there were two wicker baskets. In one Merry found a pound of candles, some half pence and an empty soda bottle which smelled of oil. The other contained two ladies' caps. Beside it, as if they had tumbled out, were a pair of ladies' mud boots wrapped in white paper. Further searching discovered the dead person's hat nearby close to a field.

Curious that robbery did not seem to be the reason for the crime, the Merrys searched for other clues. Nearby they found marks on the road three to four feet long, which seemed to suggest that the corpse had been dragged along. They also found a horse about 35 yards away, fastened to a gate. It was this vital piece of evidence which suggested that a murder had taken place.

In cross examination Charles Merry the elder insisted that the animal was completely tied to the gate. The bridle was thrown over two or three bars of the gate, something which a horse could not have done itself. Also, Charles was amazed that the horse had bridle and saddle but no stirrups.

When Charles Merry the younger gave evidence he also was adamant that the animal was fastened. Mr Lee, the prosecutor, asked rather flippantly "Have you always told the same story about the transaction?" to which Charles, very annoyed, answered, "Story sir – it's no story. The bridle was not loosely over the gate!".Charles's reaction to the question brought laughter from the gallery, but his straight denial that it was a story was noted by judge and jury.

Rumours circulating in the area a few weeks after the crime had suggested that the horse was not tied, and they had led Charles the elder to visit the Coroner, Sir John Fowler. Charles told him of the stories and asked to see his deposition to make sure it had been written correctly, since he had not had it read back to him. Having seen the statement, he went away satisfied.

When the Merrys found the body the son had raced to one nearby farmhouse for help while the father went to another. They returned with John David Greaves and a man called Banister, who brought a lantern. They all examined the body and the horse more closely. With the light shining on the corpse they could see that the man was dressed in a dark coat and striped breeches. His left hand was bandaged with binding, possibly as a result of the fight. Charles the elder raised the body and Greaves recognised it as Hollier.

The Merrys reckoned they could do no more at the scene, so left Greaves and Banister and made their way to work. Perhaps it was youthful curiosity that made young Charles Merry return to the scene later that day. The corpse and the horse had been removed, but looking around carefully Charles noticed hoof prints in the ditch near where the body was found, as well as drag marks.

So how had the horse come to be tied up 35 yards away from the corpse? Had Hollier been thrown from his mount and dragged, only to walk that distance to tie up the animal when he got his breath back? If so, why did he walk back to rest where he had fallen? And why the hoof prints in the ditch? Mystified, young Merry examined the surrounding ground but found nothing that might suggest a fight or struggle. It was those strange facts that he reported to Constable Roe and repeated to the Coroner.

When John Greaves gave his evidence, he also said he was sure that the horse had been tied. With the Merrys he had examined the corpse and found congealed blood on the bosom, together with bruises to the head, possibly from a fall or blow. The face was scratched as if the person had been dragged along the ground. When the Merrys had left and he stayed by the body with Bannister, he had told his servant to take the corpse to the New Inn for the surgeon to see.

Greaves offered a possible explanation of how the horse might have got tied. He said that it was very common for horses, when they got loose, to toss their heads over gates. The reigns could have looped themselves around the bars, but how they had knotted themselves as well he did not know.

Greaves also told the court that he knew Hollier, who was about twenty five. He was inclined to get drunk often and was in the habit of falling from his horse. The animal was so used to this behaviour that it would wait by his side until he recovered and remounted. In the countryside there are many stories of such relationships between man and horse.

But the court was still baffled as to how the animal came to be tied, and after Banister's evidence, which agreed totally with the others, no new light had been shed on the incident. Henry Wilson, gamekeeper to the Marquis of Anglesey, gave expert advice on the behaviour of horses and was adamant that it was impossible for the animal to have fastened itself.

Possible explanations did appear when the two surgeons gave their evidence, though nothing that could be concluded as indisputable fact. Neither of them had arrived at a definite conclusion about the cause of death and on some points they contradicted one another.

William Whateley, the first surgeon to examine the body, had found the face gorged with blood. It was very dark, but not from age. There had been bleeding from the nose, a mark on the mouth, scratches around the eyes and one of the front teeth was loose. In his judgement Hollier had been dead for about five hours.

At first he could find no cause for the actual death, but closer scrutiny revealed a fractured skull. There was blood on the brain which had caused Hollier's death and two apoplecile cells. These were very common in cases of apoplexy where the victim had lost consciousness due to a burst blood vessel in the brain.

So much for the straightforward science, but when asked how the victim might have suffered these injuries Whateley could only say, "It might be a fall from a horse, or a blow by a heavy weapon". He was certain there were no external marks of violence except those around the face.

The second surgeon was John Whatley, who was no relation to the differently spelt Mr Whateley. He agreed with William Whateley's finding that: "The skull was fractured in all probability from a fall", but "it might have been occasioned by a blow from a heavy instrument". However, he went on to suggest another possible cause of death. He said that Hollier might have ridden for an hour or two after a fall, which would account for the physical appearance of the corpse. Then feeling ill, Hollier might have dismounted, walked a little and then collapsed. To support his theory John Whatley added, "I have known instances of persons, after receiving blows on the head, dress themselves and walk to the hospital. Death had afterwards ensued". Like the other witnesses, he knew Hollier well and his drinking habits, and his custom of riding home when drunk. If this had happened on 13th March alcohol might have hidden the pain from a fall until he finally succumbed and collapsed.

At last the court seemed to be getting somewhere, but confusion returned when John Whatley declared that the victim had not died from apoplexy. Convinced that the trial was proving nothing and going round in circles, Mr Justice Bosanquet stopped the case. In his view it would be impossible to convict the prisoners and so he instructed the jury to find them not guilty.

That left the mystery of the tied horse. One witness, Thomas Palne, had met the prisoners near to where the body was found, but that had been at 7.30 pm when Hollier was riding alongside Haines in his wagon. Could they have followed and lain in wait? If so, why? Batkin had already beaten Hollier and won the dog, Palne swore they had it with them when he met them. Why would Batkin want to teach him a further lesson?

It is clear that some of Hollier's injuries happened in the fight at the inn. Could he have received the fractured skull during the fight, but being drunk, shrugged it off and ridden away, only to feel unwell later and collapse? That could account for the horse being tethered so far away. He could have dismounted, tied the animal and then walked before dying. But that does not account for the drag marks near the body, or the hoof prints in the ditch. Only the horse knew the exact story.

Perhaps Batkin and Shorthouse were lucky to have lived in the early 19th century. Modern medical knowledge might have found that the fight was the main cause of death, and seen them convicted of manslaughter.

Murder or Misadventure?
(Cobridge 1878 – Staffordshire Daily Sentinel)

When bringing a person before a judge and jury on a charge of murder, the police (more recently, the Crown Prosecution Service) have to be fairly certain that their case will succeed. Most probably they will have witnesses whose evidence will show the motive and circumstances, and they may have the murder weapon. But what if none of these are available? The case must rest mainly on the evidence of the surgeons. This was the situation in which the Potteries Police found themselves when John Pointon was arrested for the murder of Eliza Bloor at Cobridge, near Burslem, in 1878.

Eliza Bloor had been widowed in early 1878, and for the five months after her husband's death she had taken up with 28 year old John Pointon, a potter from Burslem. The two were on very friendly terms. Pointon was later to deny that they were courting, but they were often seen together in the St Paul's Tavern at Dalehall on Saturday evenings.

October 5th was no exception. Both were there by 8.30 pm and left at 9.30, and were seen by Constable James walking down Newcastle Street. Though obviously the worse for drink, they caused no trouble and so the officer ignored them.

At 12.00 pm the couple were seen by Abraham Clarke on the pathway that led from Cobridge to Burslem, and he was asked by Pointon for help in carrying Eliza. At first Clarke refused, but seeing the trouble Pointon was having he decided to help.

Instinct told him that something was wrong and he lit a match to see the woman. He was horrified to find that she was dead and lying in a pool of blood.

When Mr Oldham, the surgeon saw the body he found a wound that had entered the groin and passed upwards, causing bleeding. His view was that it had been caused by a knife and Eliza had died from a haemorrhage. With that evidence, the police arrested Pointon for murder.

Further examinations of the path revealed pools of blood along the way at regular intervals, suggesting that the wound had been inflicted some distance from where the corpse was found. No matter how hard they searched the police never found a knife, but Mr Oldham's insistence that murder had happened convinced the police that that they had their killer. Pointon was committed for trial at the Stafford Assizes.

In the meantime the Eliza Bloor case gained such notoriety that visitors came far and wide to look at the scene of the murder. And as visitors looked, locals gave their theories about poor Eliza's death.

Supporters of Pointon proclaimed that the couple were very happy and never argued. At the inquest, Pointon had seemed so relaxed that even the Coroner was surprised. Was that how a murderer would behave? And would a murderer ask for help in carrying his victim?

Pointon's opponents argued that he had deliberately chosen such a lonely spot to seduce Eliza, and when she refused him, he killed her. And he didn't love her because when she talked of them marrying he denied all knowledge of the suggestion. He was only out for what he could get – a truly callous murderer.

The trial opened before Mr Justice Fry in January 1879 with Mr Brindley prosecuting and Mr Underhill for the defence. Speculation should have ended in the courtroom, but the unfolding proceedings led to more. In fact speculation went on refreshed after the trial because there was so little concrete evidence to offer the jury. Mr Brindley began by suggesting that there was indeed a motive for murder, but the more he questioned witnesses the more doubt there seemed to be.

Mrs Margaret Ford's deposition was read to the jury because she had died in the months before the trial. She had been the landlady of the St Paul's Tavern and knew both Bloor and Pointon. On the evening of Saturday, 5th October, John Pointon had been in her bar alone from about 7.30 and had

had one drink. At about 8 o'clock, he had asked Ann Eardley to fetch Eliza. When she arrived the two remained in the bar until about 9.30 pm when they left together. Pointon had drunk two or three glasses of beer and Eliza two. When they left the couple had seemed on friendly terms.

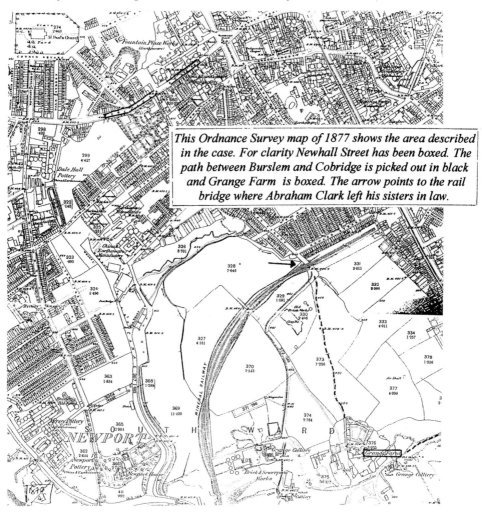

This Ordnance Survey map of 1877 shows the area described in the case. For clarity Newhall Street has been boxed. The path between Burslem and Cobridge is picked out in black and Grange Farm is boxed. The arrow points to the rail bridge where Abraham Clark left his sisters in law.

Even so, Mrs Ford had said that Eliza seemed "so down". When she had questioned her about it, the deceased had said that she and Pointon were to be married, but Pointon was unwilling to set a date. But Mrs Ford added that the two never argued about it and always seemed very friendly.

Ann Eardley, the next witness, lived in Bag Street, Dalehall and knew Eliza Bloor, who had lived in the same street. On the evening in question John Pointon had asked her where Eliza was. When Ann replied that she was at home, Pointon asked her to fetch Eliza. She had done so and found Eliza complaining of a headache, but she still washed and changed and followed Ann to the pub. During their stay there the couple were on friendly terms.

So far Mr Brindley had produced no prosecution witness who had seen the couple arguing, but had their friendly mood changed after they left the tavern? There was little evidence that it did.

Mary Ann Eardley, daughter of the previous witness, said that she had been on her way home from Burslem at about 10 o'clock on the Saturday evening when she met the couple. She had walked with them from Foundry Lane to Furlong Passage when Eliza suggested that she and Pointon turn back. Pointon wanted to go a little further and Eliza agreed. Mary had left as they continued towards Grange Fields but she was sure that both were still friendly.

Other witnesses, including Constable James, testified to seeing the couple walking towards Grange Fields that evening. All but one agreed that everything seemed fine except that they might have had a little too much to drink.

William George Rowley, a young potter, was walking along Enoch Street when he noticed a couple in an entry arguing, and he thought they might have been Bloor and Pointon. He told the court that he heard the prisoner say to the Eliza Bloor, "Ar't going?" to which she had replied, "Not if hell fire had you!"

Mr Brindley quickly latched on to this, suggesting that an argument had developed which led to murder. Pointon's aim throughout the walk along Newcastle Street and further had been to lure Eliza into the deserted area around Grange Fields, where he hoped to seduce her. When he had got her there but failed in his attempt, he murdered her.

Mr Brindley found it difficult to support this theory. Witnesses who saw the couple in Grange Fields did not see any misdoings. John Parr said that on that Saturday evening he had gone for a walk up Grange Fields with Mary Hancock. When they reached as far as Grange Farm, at about 10.40, they had turned back. On coming down Grange Fields they had seen the couple on the footpath. The woman was lying down and the man was standing about one yard away. As they got nearer Pointon had said to him, "Jack, do you know her?", referring to the dead woman. When he said that he did not Pointon said that it was Eliza Bloor.

Cross examined by Mr Underhill, Counsel for the Defence, Parr admitted that Pointon may have added that the deceased suffered from fits, but he could not be certain. However, Mary Hancock remembered that she had asked Pointon herself about fits, and he had replied that Eliza did suffer from them.

James Baker of Lower Hadderidge, Burslem, said that on the Saturday night he was coming from Hanley at about 10.15 with a young woman. They had turned at Cobridge to come across Grange Fields when they saw a couple lying in the pathway. The woman was lying flat on the ground and the man was stretched across the road with his back resting on a rail. Nothing was said and they passed by. He had presumed that everything was fine, except for drink.

The last person to see the couple was Abraham Clarke who lived opposite the Grange Farm that was owned by his father. He had left home some time between 11 and 12 twelve o'clock to walk his sisters in law back to Burslem. On their way they came across a man and woman lying in the path some five or six yards from the farm entrance. The man was sitting but the woman was lying full length, her head resting on the man's arms. Clarke noticed a pool of liquid surrounding the woman, but it was too dark to see clearly what it really was.

He left his sisters in law at the railway bridge then returned along the path. As he reached the couple the man called him to help carry the woman, but at first he refused. However, he changed his mind and soon realised that the woman was dead. When he told Pointon all he said was, "What must I do with her?"

Clarke raced back to the farm for help, leaving the prisoner with the body. When he returned with his father and another man, Pointon had disappeared and so he went to find the police. As he got to Waterloo Road he met the prisoner with Constable James and Sergeant Hughes. Clarke immediately told the officers that a woman had been murdered and even accused Pointon of being the murderer, to which the prisoner made no reply. Clarke offered to take the officers to the scene, but before going there they all went to collect the police surgeon.

Clarke said that during examination of the corpse, both at the scene and at the hotel, Pointon seemed quite sober and even "smoked his pipe coolly". When cross examined by Mr Underhill, Clarke added that throughout these initial examinations Pointon had acted as though the woman were not dead, even appearing quite casual.

31

The prosecution focused on that casual approach to the death when questioning the police officers, hoping to show the jury that they were dealing with a callous man who showed no compassion, even for the woman he was supposed to love.

Constable James gave evidence that he had been in Newcastle Street near Furlong Place at about 12 o'clock when he saw Pointon walking very quickly towards Dalehall. He stopped the man and asked after the woman who had been with him. Pointon had said, quite matter of factly, "You know the woman you saw me with at Dalehall? She has just dropped dead in my arms up by the Grange Farm."

James asked the prisoner if he had called for a doctor, to which the Pointon replied that he was going to fetch Eliza Bloor's brother first. The constable told the jury that Pointon had seemed out of breath and excited, but he had put that down to him running very fast. He added that when he asked Pointon to come with him to the scene, the prisoner made no resistance and went quietly.

Sergeant Hughes told the court that he had been patrolling St John's Square when Constable James arrived with the prisoner and reported what Pointon had said. On their way to collect Mr Oldham, the surgeon, they met Abraham Clarke, and they all went to Grange Farm where they found the corpse. When he asked Pointon if the woman had complained of being ill before the tragedy, the prisoner had said that she had not.

A preliminary survey of the scene showed blood on the pathway and all over the body. After Mr Oldham had examined the body and told Sergeant Hughes of his finding, the sergeant arrested Pointon for causing the death of Eliza Bloor. He searched the prisoner and found money, a box of matches, two pipes, a twist of tobacco and three pledge tickets. There was no knife. On his arrest, the prisoner had said, "I never touched her if I must die".

If lack of any clear motive for murder was damaging to the prosecution's case, then failure to produce the murder weapon was serious. The following day the police had searched the area thoroughly but found nothing. Chief Inspector Longdon told the court that they had found quantities of blood in patches stretching from the railway bridge to Grange Farm, a distance of about three hundred yards, which suggested that the deceased had walked or been carried so far and then been rested or placed down. Despite days of searching and inquiries, no knife was ever found, but Pointon had had many opportunities to throw it away.

Mr Underhill, for the Defence, suggested to the court that there had never been a knife and that Eliza had accidentally sat down upon some sharp object which had punctured her groin. To try to prove his argument, Mr Dain, a Burslem architect, was called. He told the jury that the path was formed of ashes, but it was not a particularly rough road. However, it was in such a place that discarded, broken pottery might be found.

To press his point Mr Underhill produced evidence that Pointon never carried a knife, that evening or at any time. A witness named Davenport said that Pointon had borrowed a knife from him in St Paul's Tavern on the evening of 5th October to cut up some tobacco twist. When Davenport asked him why he did not have his own knife, Pointon had said "I never carry one". Another witness, John Durber, a sagger maker for whom Pointon had worked, said that he often had to lend Pointon a knife as the prisoner never carried one.

[**A sagger,** for non Potteries readers, is a fireclay container, oval or round in shape in which unfired wares would be placed to protect them from flames and smoke in the kiln.]

With motive and the murder weapon seriously in doubt, Mr Brindley's case was faltering. Even so, but he still had the evidence of Mr Oldham, the surgeon, to show that Eliza had suffered a wound which was difficult to explain without a murderous blow.

Mr Oldham said that when he examined the body at the Queen's Hotel, the corpse and clothing were covered in blood and in a shocking state, but there was no evidence of external wounds. Closer examination had revealed a distinct incised wound an inch and a half long extending from the pubic base, and about three quarters of an inch deep. It had severed the pubic artery and other arteries, which accounted for the loss of blood. At the Coroner's request he had made a post mortem examination on Monday 7th October and come to the conclusion that the wound was caused by a well defined, sharp instrument like a knife.

"Life a knife" was the point on which Mr Underhill cross examined the surgeon, suggesting that the wound had been caused not by a knife, but by a sharp piece of pottery. Mr Oldham insisted that pottery shards would only cause lacerated wounds and not clearly defined ones. Lacerated wounds, Mr Oldham argued, though they would cause bleeding, would never cause the amount found at the scene. Only clear cut wounds would produce such a profusion of blood.

The technical argument did not convince Mr Underhill. He asked why the surgeon had refused a second opinion, despite Pointon's father requesting one. Mr Oldham replied that he had never been told of the request. On Mr Underhill's insistence Inspector Longdon was re-examined and said that to his knowledge, Pointon's father had not made such a request. If he had then there would certainly have been a second post mortem.

To bolster his case, Mr Brindley recalled Mr Oldham and the surgeon reaffirmed his evidence. He added that a second post mortem could have proved little about the type of wounds inflicted because when he had performed the first one, he had to cut away large portions of the groin to make a thorough examination.

With the prosecution case complete Mr Underhill opted not to put Pointon onto the stand or call further evidence, and so the barristers were left to make their closing speeches.

Mr Brindley, his case severely weakened, made a great issue of the scene where Eliza's body was found. He said it was a place notorious for immoral acts and when Pointon could not have his way, he had murdered the poor woman. He also maintained that the surgeon was the only expert in the case and he was definite that murder had been committed.

Mr Underhill relied heavily on the fact that no motive for murder had been proved, quite the opposite. The couple always seemed perfectly happy in one another's company. As for the supposed weapon and its disappearance, its absence only proved that there never had been such a weapon. As for the wound, only an expert on human anatomy would be able to inflict such a precise wound, and that would only be possible if the victim did not struggle.

In his summing up Mr Justice Fry, told the jury that an obvious motive was not always present in murder cases because there was such a thing as a crime of passion. As to the knife, Pointon could have disposed of it as he had the opportunity while alone on the pathway before he met Constable James. However, the judge told the jury, the deciding factor in proving innocence or guilt was the wound. Could a man like the prisoner inflict such a wound and in such a place, knowing its consequences, or was he simply fortunate? Finally, he had to point out that the prisoner could have removed the body from the scene, as there were plenty of places to hide it, but he did not.

It took only five minutes for the jury to decide that Pointon was not guilty and he walked free from the court, but speculation still spun giddily around the Potteries. Many people believed that Pointon had got away with a very callous murder.

In an interview with a reporter from the *Daily Sentinel* on Monday 2nd February 1879 Pointon said, "I knew nothing whatever about the wound or the cause of her death. I wasn't in the least bit frightened because I had done nothing and knew they wouldn't do anything to me. They (the prison authorities) let all my friends come to see me. They all seemed to think I should be hung, but I never thought so."

Murder,
Manslaughter or Accident?
(Bilston 1890 – Express & Star)

The balance of the human mind is a delicate thing; upset that equilibrium and even the most sane person may do desperate things. English criminal law has long recognised that a crime consists of two elements, a physical act such as a killing or taking someone's property, and a mental element, such as intention, carelessness or dishonesty. It is common sense that if someone's mind was disturbed it throws doubt on whether they intended the consequence of their acts.

Our criminal law has always understood the idea that the `insane' could not form the necessary intention, though its definition of insanity describes such an extreme form of mania that very few people are ever likely to suffer from it. The law had much more difficulty with disturbed states of mind falling short of actual insanity, and did not really recognise them until well into the 20th century.

Certainly the mind of John Wyse was terribly disturbed during the events leading to his trial 1890, when he was charged with the murder of Mary Davies, a friend and the wife to his closest friend, James Davies.

When he appeared before Mr Justice Matthew at Stafford Assizes on 16th December 1890 the officials, the lawyers, the jury and the public saw a man in total despair. Asked how he pleaded, Wyse muttered "Guilty", but hung his head in shame. As the proceedings went on it became obvious that he was suffering greatly. The *Express and Star* reporter wrote that "bitter tears flowed" and "the poor fellow buried his face in a handkerchief and became absolutely helpless under the power of his sorrow". Such was his remorse that "he was an object of commiseration to all around, and those present felt deeply for him".

John Wyse was a thirty five year old steel fitter who lived with his wife and four children at Meadow Lane in Sedgeley. The couple had been married for close on eleven years and everything seemed perfectly happy. John was a good husband and devoted father who worked hard to keep his family. His habits were very sober and he wanted nothing more than to care for his family and provide them with the best home he could afford.

Unfortunately his wife, who was not named in the trial, did not share the same devotion towards John, and she began an affair with Jim Davies, the young son of James and Mary Davies, Wyse's best friends. John Wyse seemed to have had no suspicions and so was totally devastated when his wife eloped with Jim Davies on 23rd August 1890, taking with her the youngest child and all of her clothing.

Beside himself with grief, Wyse questioned his neighbour, Mrs Butler, but even if she knew of the affair she did not say. However, she promised to look after the remaining children while John searched for his wife. On Monday 25th August he visited Langman's Pawnshop in Dudley Street, Wolverhampton and bought a revolver, before setting off for Liverpool where he thought the pair might be. Fortunately he never found them and returned home the following day.

Determined to seek them out, he went to the Davies's house to find out if they knew anything. He was sure Mary Davies had relatives in Yorkshire and the Potteries where the couple might be hiding. As he walked towards the Davies's home, he met James Davies who offered to help. He escorted

36

Wyse to the house to talk with Mary. She either did not know anything or would not admit to the pair's whereabouts, and Wyse became very agitated. During their conversation he produced the revolver and fired it, and Mary Davies was mortally wounded. Realising what he had done, Wyse turned the gun on himself.

In some respects, the jury had an easy decision. There was no disputing who had shot Mary Davies. But was it murder? Had John Wyse gone to the house with the intention of killing someone? Had he formed such an intention while he was there? If he had threatened Mary Davies with the gun just intending to frighten her then he might be guilty of manslaughter. Or was it an accident?

Most remarkable in the case was the evidence given by James Davies, Mary's husband. Those in court might have expected total condemnation of the prisoner, but they heard exactly the opposite. James Davies had nothing bad to say about Wyse. He told the court that they had been close friends "from the cradle", and that John Wyse was "a hard working and industrious man" who was very fond of his family. The elopement had destroyed his friend who could not comprehend it because, in James's words, John Wyse "was one of the best husbands in the world".

Describing the events that led up to the shooting, Davies told the court that he had been walking towards his home in Hidding's Lane, Deepfields, with his brother, Henry, when they had met John Wyse. His friend was in a very distraught state, saying that he had been to Liverpool in search of his wife. Wanting to help Wyse, James took him to Hidding's Lane to see his wife, Mary. Henry went to his home to fetch his wife, Betsy, and they both came to the Davies's house.

James insisted that during the conversation that took place, Wyse never quarrelled with any of them even though he was most distressed. He had asked Mary for addresses in Yorkshire and the Potteries and had said of his trip to Liverpool, "If I could a' met wi' em they'd a both been jed [dead] uns. I should have served me both like that". As Wyse finished speaking, he pulled out the gun and fired it at Mary. Realising that his wife had been shot, James grabbed hold of her and dragged her outside. While there, he heard two more shots from inside the house.

Henry Davies and his wife, Betsy, both agreed with James Davies's evidence, adding only that Wyse seemed so distressed at what had happened that he had shot himself in the side. While Mary Davies was being taken to a nearby tavern they had laid Wyse out on the sofa and then summoned the police.

Sergeant Ellis told the court that he had arrived at the house at about 3.40 pm and found John Wyse on the sofa. When he asked the prisoner what he had done, his reply was, "Oh Lord, have mercy on me. It's them going off and leaving me with three children." Ellis found the revolver on the sofa and asked the prisoner if there were any more bullets, to which the prisoner replied, "I have no more bullets. I changed it for them, James Davies's wife and my wife. Them poor little children. They all knew about it but they did not lead me into the light of it".

These words are not easy to understand but the prosecution made much of them. In his final speech to the jury Counsel interpreted it as an admission that Wyse had deliberately killed Mary Davies.

Sergeant Ellis said that he had asked questions about the purchase of the gun, but was interrupted by Edward Davies, another brother, entering the room. When the prisoner saw Edward he said, "There's Ted, you're lucky." What did he mean? Not long after that the prisoner fell into a sleep. The following day he was taken to hospital where he stayed for a month.

Constable Tittensor had accompanied Sergeant Ellis to the scene and stayed with the prisoner all night. He told the court that when he had asked the prisoner about the bullets, Wyse told him that he had only bought six. He had fired the missing one in Knox's Field close to his home to see if they were good. Damning evidence, as it showed that Wyse had intended to shoot someone. But was it Mary Davies? Wyse was so desperate and confused that it could have been anyone.

The one witness who could throw some light on his state of mind was Sarah Butler, his next door neighbour. She said that on 23rd August John Wyse came to her house and had obviously been crying. He told her of his wife's disappearance and said that he thought that she might be at her mother's in Walsall. He had asked her to mind the children while he was away. The following day, Sunday, he had again asked her to mind the children, telling her that he had been to Bilston to take out a warrant for his wife's arrest because she had taken the youngest child.

When Sarah Butler had gone into Wyse's house she found him still crying. He told her that he had had no sleep since last Thursday. She had persuaded him to lie down, but by the following morning he had left for Liverpool.

38

When questioned Sarah Butler said that she had known on Saturday, 23rd August that Mrs Wyse and young Jim Davies had eloped. On the Friday, Saturday and Tuesday when she saw the prisoner, he had been in a terribly distressed state of mind. She said that he "was perfectly distracted about the children being left, about his own destitution, and his wife having stripped the house".

Sarah knew her neighbour well and would be expected to know what a state he was in. But a total stranger had also noticed Wyse's distressed behaviour.

Frederick King was the assistant to Mr Langton, a pawnbroker who had sold the revolver to Wyse on Monday 25th August. King told the jury that there was something odd about the customer's demeanour which had led him to say, "I hope you are not going to shoot yourself". It was only when the prisoner had assured him that he would not that King handed over the revolver for 12s 6d. [62.5p]

King also told the jury that Wyse seemed to know nothing about guns because he "appeared to be totally ignorant of the proper way to handle such a weapon". When told that he could not purchase bullets at their shop, the prisoner seemed anxious and confused until King directed him to the ironmongers. At Cozens & Shaw's shop Wyse had to produce the revolver before the assistant could tell him what bullets he needed.

On the surface these events might not seem strange, but Mr Young for the defence was to suggest that Wyse's lack of knowledge of firearms was to prove accidentally fatal for Mary Davies. Not realising how easy it was to fire such a weapon, Wyse had accidentally pulled the trigger while pointing it at Mrs Davies.

It was that argument and Wyse's obviously distraught state of mind which Mr Young relied on. He was to argue that John Wyse had been a man of unblemished character, the perfect husband and loving father, but his wife's actions had caused him to act outside his normal character. "He went about hardly knowing what he did, hardly knowing what he was talking about, unable to sleep, unable to eat, and unable to bear the mention of his wife and children." He had even told Sarah Butler that he was "too ashamed to go out" in case people blamed him for his wife's behaviour.

It was that distressed state of mind, Mr Young argued, which led his client to act foolishly and produce the revolver at the Davies's home, and that state of mind which made him accidentally pull the trigger. That explained what he might do if he ever saw his wife and Jim Davies again; a sort of bravado. It went off accidentally when, unfortunately, it was pointing at Mrs Davies.

Probably it was James Davies's evidence, the sorry state of Wyse as he stood in the dock and Mr Young's closing arguments, which led the jury to dismiss the charge of wilful murder. They found him guilty of manslaughter, presumably concluding that Mary Davies had been killed as a result of his unlawful act of threatening or trying to frighten her. Even so, they made a strong plea to the judge to show mercy.

Mr Justice Mathew was bound by law to impose some form of punishment, but he agreed with the jury that the prisoner had suffered enough distress in having to live with what he had done. He sentenced Wyse to six days imprisonment, but as he had already been in custody for longer than that he was discharged immediately.

Whether Wyse ever saw his wife again is not known, but he left the court a broken man. Only his love for his children would help him survive.

Birdcage Talk
(Hanley 1897 – Staffs Sentinel)

The chances of relating the exact words of a conversation without adding the odd word or missing some out are almost nil, yet witnesses are expected to do this. A defendant's whole future may rely on the witness's memory. But what if that witness might already be influenced by his or her relationship with the prisoner?

Margaret Day lived with her daughter, Clara, and husband Christopher Styles, at 4, Cross Street, Hanley. On the Friday afternoon of 27th August 1897 both women decided to visit Margaret's son, William. When they arrived at 10 Birdcage Walk, Hanley, they found William at home with his wife, Jenny, and brother, Henry Bonor Day.

Happy to see one another, the family soon began to swap gossip. It was during that time that William took down two revolvers from the wall and began to show them off to his mother, explaining that they had bought them for rabbit shooting. At some point William pointed one of his guns at his mother's head and pulled the trigger several times. Unfortunately, on the third pull the revolver fired, killing Margaret instantly.

Terrified at what he had done, William rushed out of the house to find a doctor, but in his panic he went first to a Mr Jones, the local dentist. Eventually he got to Dr Broadbent's, but by the time they returned to Birdcage Walk it was too late. The police were called and William gave himself up. At the police station he was charged with causing the death of his mother.

HANLEY REVOLVER FATALITY.

BEFORE THE MAGISTRATES.

SERIOUS DEVELOPMENT.

FURTHER REMAND.

As usual The Sentinel refuses to get excited. Note the full stops, which you don't see in modern headlines.

A death under such circumstances has to be treated with suspicion and an inquest held. The Coroner assembled a jury at Hanley Town Hall on Monday 30th August to decide whether William had deliberately killed his mother or whether it was just a terrible accident. It promised to be a straightforward enquiry until witnesses began to contradict one another.

Clara Styles, William's sister, said that she had arrived with her mother to visit William and family, but when the actual shooting took place she was in the yard at the back of the house. She had been there above five minutes before she heard the shot. Rushing into the house she found her mother still seated, but with a bullet hole in her head.

Her brother was in a state of panic and when she asked him what had happened he blurted out, "Clara, I have done it!" She asked him why he had shot his mother and William said, "I've done it for nothing. Go and fetch a doctor." But she insisted that he get the doctor. When he got back to Birdcage Walk he had waited by the fireplace for the police to arrive.

Questioned as to William's exact words and their possible meaning, Clara became flustered and several times changed her mind. Her second version became, "Clara, I've murdered my mother", which brought gasps from the assembled hearing. Whether Clara realised the importance of what she had said or not the court would never know, because she quickly altered her rendering to, "Clara, I've accidentally murdered my mother."

Unsure that Clara was a safe witness, the jury began to question her more thoroughly. What was the precise mood of the people present before she went into the yard? Clara was insistent that everyone was happy, there had been "no quarrel at all", and that as far as she was concerned "everything was perfectly quiet and peaceful".

There was some doubt as to whether the front door was locked or unlocked. Could it be that William had locked it to stop anyone entering before he committed the deed? Clara was positive that the door was unlocked, though it did sometimes stick.

Clara was obviously becoming frightened and bewildered by the constant questions, or perhaps by her own answers. At this point the Coroner stopped what was turning into harassment. Even so, before she stepped down Clara told the jury that she distinctly remembered Jenny Day saying, "Oh Clara, Bill's accidentally murdered his mother."

If the jury were confused by Clara Styles' evidence, their next witness was to muddy the waters even further. Alfred McIvor lived at 6 Birdcage Walk. He said that at about 4 o'clock on that Friday afternoon he was in his house when he heard a report like that of a firearm. He ran towards number 10 and was met by William Day, who had just managed to open the front door. When he asked William what had happened, the prisoner said, "I've shot my mother in place of Jenny."

Once again there were gasps from the courtroom, but McIvor went on. William ran off towards Broad Street and he went into number 10 to see what had happened. He found Clara Styles, Jenny Day, a young man whom he did not know holding two revolvers, and Margaret Day dead in a chair.

This was shock evidence. Had William shot his mother while trying to kill his wife? If McIvor's statement was true, then the court was looking at manslaughter at the least. What followed astounded the jury even further. Mr Ashmail representing William Day began to question the integrity of McIvor.

During the questioning it started to look as though Alfred McIvor might harbour some grudge against the Day family. During that August Mrs McIvor had been in court for unruly behaviour towards her neighbours and was sentenced to seven days in prison. William Day's wife, Jenny, had been the complainant.

Curiously, McIvor insisted that he knew nothing of his wife's arrest, despite being almost ridiculed by Mr Ashmail. He even claimed that it bore no relevance to the present case. Questioned further, he became very aggressive and started to deliberately mumble his answers. Annoyed, the Coroner insisted that McIvor talk properly, or if he could not, then "Birdcage Talk" would suffice.

Insulted by the Coroner's attack on his local dialect, McIvor became more aggressive, but it gave Mr Ashmail his opportunity. He asked McIvor, because he was "not in the habit" of using "Birdcage Talk" as he spoke words "as plain as anyone else", if he might have mistaken William Day's "Birdcage Talk" of "in the face of Jenny" and heard "in the place of Jenny".

Angry that Mr Ashmail might be mocking him, McIvor insisted that he had clearly heard William say "in the place of Jenny" and, turning to the Coroner, professed that he had come to that court determined not "to tell a lot of lies".

What should have been a straightforward case was turning into a nightmare. They had one frightened witness who might change her evidence each time she was questioned, and another so aggressive that he was proving hostile.

Perhaps their third witness might be more helpful? She was Mary Day, but no relation to the Day family. From the start of her testimony it was clear to the jury that things were going to get worse. Mary Day lived at 8 Birdcage Walk, but at the time of the "murder" (her word) she had lived at number 6, McIvor's house. The Coroner stopped her immediately to point out that it was the court's duty to decide if the crime was indeed murder.

Mary Day went on unabashed. She said that she had heard a noise like a gun going off and had run into the street. From there she had heard William Day unlocking his front door with his key and saw him come outside. She clearly remembered him saying, "I have shot my mother in mistake for Jenny".

Once again the court was shocked, but when Mr Ashmail began to cross examine Mary Day it soon became obvious that she also might be biased. In fact she was McIvor's daughter. Like her stepfather, she denied knowing anything of her mother's summons or the parties involved. She even denied seeing her stepfather in the street outside number 10 talking to William Day, yet how did he pass her and go into the house? Like McIvor, she insisted that all she had told the court was truthful.

Was the court to believe her? Perhaps the fourth witness would be more credible. William's brother, Henry Bonor Day, was brought before the court with a police escort because he was an army deserter. He said that when his mother and sister had arrived at Birdcage Walk he was seated examining an object taken out of pawn that morning. It was he who had pointed to the two revolvers on the wall over the mantelpiece and William had taken one down to show his mother. He was sure that both his mother and brother were laughing and joking when William pointed the revolver at her head and pulled the trigger.

Henry had told William not to be so silly, but his mother seemed quite unperturbed. It was when he pulled the trigger for the third time that it fired. When William realised what had happened, he ran from the house to get a doctor, the gun had dropped to the floor and Henry had picked it up and put it on the table. Then, realising that the police would arrive at any minute and remembering that he was a deserter, he ran away.

When Mr Ashmail questioned him Henry insisted that the family were in a happy mood and that there had been no quarrelling. As to how the revolver came to have a cartridge in it, Henry was adamant that the man who sold them the gun had tried cartridges in them to show them how they were loaded. When they got home they simply took the revolvers out of their wrapping and hung them on the wall.

Could that have happened? Arthur James Tatton, manager of an ironmongers firm at Longton, said that he had sold a revolver to two men, the prisoner being one, at 1 o'clock on the Friday afternoon. They had said that they wanted it for rabbit shooting. They paid 23s 6d [£1.17] for it and some cartridges. There were fifty cartridges in the box, but Tatton was positive that he had not loaded the gun as the men had not asked him how it was loaded. He was certain that the revolver was empty when he sold it.

The second gun they bought at Messrs Palfreyman's, the pawnbrokers, on the Friday morning. Again, the assistant was certain that he had not loaded the gun and that it was empty at the time of purchase. Also John Pepper, an assistant at Smith Bros of Hanley, testified that he had sold some cartridges to the prisoner that same Friday.

The Coroner was interested to note that all three salesmen were quite happy to sell their items to the men as they seemed "honest" and genuine sports-men. That same integrity was affirmed by Mr Jones, the dentist that William Day had rushed to on the fatal afternoon. He said that the prisoner had arrived in an excited state saying that he had shot his mother accidentally. He could not help and had directed the prisoner to the doctor's.

The Coroner had only one question for Mr Jones. "Did you think the man was telling you a true tale?", to which Mr Jones replied, "At the time I really thought that it was an accident. He seemed to be very much put out by what had occurred."

Even the police admitted that William seemed genuinely sorry for what had happened. He had openly admitted to killing his mother and had gone quietly with Constable Harris to the station where he was charged. Only a couple of things had concerned the police. Firstly, they had found the revolvers in the washhouse boiler half covered in water, secondly, they had found one box of cartridges with its lid opened. But these facts might be explained after further questioning of witnesses.

All evidence finished for the time being, the Coroner summed up the case. He concluded that various statements might prove difficult to believe and should be treated with care. Margaret Day had been killed and her son, William, was responsible, but to what degree? Was it a crime of murder, had William been reckless and so guilty of manslaughter, or was just a tragic accident?

It took the jury only ten minutes to reach a unanimous verdict of accidental death and they hoped that the Magistrates' Court, to be held shortly, would agree with their decision.

When the Magistrates' Court met on Thursday 2nd September, there were three main areas of contention which had to be resolved before William Day might be set free or sent to the Assizes at Stafford. Firstly, what exactly had he said to various people after the shooting? Secondly, was the door to number 10 locked, and if so, why? Thirdly, who had placed the cartridge in the revolver? The answer to the last question could go a long way to proving murder or at least manslaughter.

The case for wilful murder seemed to have been dropped from the outset, though Mr Richardson for the prosecution never dismissed it completely. He preferred to argue the case for manslaughter, arguing that William Day should never have pointed the revolver at his mother.

McIvor and Mary Day were called again and once more, repeated their versions of the conversations with the prisoner. Along with these two witnesses, the prosecution produced Martha Davies who lived at 12 Birdcage Walk. She testified that the prisoner had said, "I have catched my mother instead of Jenny", before he ran off towards the dentist's house.

Perhaps this third witness, unrelated to the McIvors, might prove decisive? Mr Ashmail, once more acting for the Defence, set about discrediting all three. McIvor's grievances against the Days were reiterated, while Mary Day had to suffer the indignity of being cross examined over her own previous jail sentences. Even Martha Davies was not spared. She had sworn that she was married to Mr Davies, but it soon was proved that her real husband was a Mr Cartledge.

Mr Ashmail's aim was to show that all three witnesses were unsafe because they all had something to hide. But the most damaging fact that came to light was that McIvor and Mary Day were left alone at the police station having tea before they made their statements to the police.

The question of the locked or unlocked door was never used to suggest that the prisoner might have planned his vile actions, rather to prove his truthfulness and the witnesses' powers of observation. However, when the police testified that the door was indeed noisy to open, whether locked or not, the whole incident was seen as irrelevant and dismissed from the case.

That left the tricky question of the loaded gun.

Once again, Mr Tatton the ironmonger swore that he never showed the two men how to load the cartridges and that the revolver was empty when he sold it to them. He also insisted that the box of cartridges was still sealed when he handed it over.

However, Joseph Gromsley, assistant in the pawnbroker's shop, did throw some light on that point. He stated that the two brothers opened the box while in his shop and showed him the cartridges to check if they were suitable for the revolver they had bought. He could not be sure if there were any missing from the box of fifty.

At that point in the proceedings there was some argument as to whether Henry Bonor Day should be called. Mr Richardson refused to call him for the prosecution as he argued that as an army deserter he was an unsafe witness. Mr Ashmail insisted that he would because Henry Bonor Day was the only person to have actually witnessed the event. Eventually he was called and apart from describing the shooting again, insisted that Mr Tatton had placed a cartridge in the revolver, but could not be sure if he had removed it afterwards.

It was that issue of the loading of the revolver which led the Magistrates to decide that William had a case to answer and should be sent to trial at Stafford. `Serious doubt' they said, meant they had to commit him on the capital charge and leave it to the judge and jury to say whether or not they would reduce it to a minor charge.

On 6th December 1897 William Day appeared at Stafford Assizes charged with the manslaughter of his mother; the murder charge had been dropped. The jury had to decide whether or not he was guilty of culpable negligence in not examining the revolver before he pointed it at his mother. The same witnesses gave the same evidence and the much the same arguments were put.

In his summing up Mr Justice Lawrence remarked to the jury that when he had first seen the revolver, he had thought that it was unloaded and even when he had held it, he was amazed to find that there was a spent cartridge in the barrel. The gun had seemed too light to be holding anything.

Did that apparently innocuous statement sway the jury? No one knows, but the jury found William Day not guilty of manslaughter and he was discharged.

Hanley Town Hall.

The Trouble with Tall Stories
(Hednesford 1896 – Express & Star)

Tall stories are expected from fishermen, but all of us at some time will exaggerate. It swells our sense of importance and often helps us become members of the gang. But even the most ardent of braggers will draw the line at topics likely to lead them into serious trouble with the law. So why did young James Lunt feel the need to involve himself in a possible murder?

On the evening of Saturday 14th November 1896 Catherine Dooley, an eighty year old pauper who lodged at Moreton Street, Chadsmoor just north of Cannock, was drinking in the Anglesey Hotel, Hednesford. At 10 o'clock the barman, Edward Poole, noted that she seemed quite sober, but by 11 o'clock, she needed someone to take her home.

As she set off that way she was met by Henry Freeman, a 38 year old joiner, who had been in the hotel's tap room. As he was heading in the same direction he offered to help her. His journey with the old lady must have been difficult because several people stopped to offer help. Just after 11 pm William Fountain met the pair near the railway bridge and he carried Catherine's umbrella and satchel while Freeman held her up.

Minutes later, because Fountain was going a different way, William Spooner took the satchel and umbrella and walked with them. He left when John Fowler, a 21 year old miner, and Joseph Platt, a 31 year old miner, caught up with the group. It was this party of four which Constable Taylor met at High Town Road. Satisfied that the old lady was in safe hands, he continued on his rounds.

Unfortunately, events proved the constable wrong. As the group reached Lees Common Catherine was suddenly thrown headlong over the hawthorn hedge, then beaten as she lay in the grass. What prompted the violent assault remained a mystery, even after the trial. Certainly it could not have been robbery because the old woman had little or no money.

Whatever the reason, the group of men involved had no chance of escaping detection because too many people had seen the old lady thrown over the hedge. What had to be decided was, which of the three men beat her and brought about her death. He may not have intended to kill her, but poor Catherine lay there so long after the attack that she must have died from exposure. It was two whole days before her body was found some distance away in a small hollow near a brook.

So far the various accounts of the incident had made no mention of young James Lunt, and had it not been for his own bragging, they never would. He was nowhere near the incident on the Saturday evening; he had not even been in the Anglesey Hotel. So why was he arrested on Friday 25th November and charged with being an accessory to the crime?

Lunt worked in the blacksmith's shop at No. 1 Pit, West Cannock Colliery close to where the attack had taken place. On Sunday 15th November he got to work to about 8.30 am desperate to tell his workmates his dreadful story. He began to tell Edward Millington about a woman's body that he had seen "in the cutting at the back of No. 3 Pit".

The Anglesey Hotel is now offices but it was built in 1831 as a hunting lodge for the Earl of Anglesey, who owned Cannock Chase.

Curious as to whether Lunt was lying or just joking, Millington asked him if he had been to tell the police. When Lunt said he hadn't, Millington wanted to be taken to where the body was supposed to be. Cornered, Lunt immediately changed his story; the woman was not really dead but alive, as she had sat up in front of him. He foolishly added that he had helped her to her feet and she seemed perfectly able to continue on her way home.

Questioned further by Millington, Lunt said that he had walked to work that morning with Henry Freeman who had told him all about the incident near Lees Common the evening before. Freeman had said that he confided in Lunt because "your mate saw it and will tell you if I don't".

Unfortunately, Lunt had assumed that Freeman was talking about Millington and had made up the story about finding the body to seem more knowledgeable than his workmate. Lunt's tall tale somehow got back to Freeman, especially the part about Catherine still being alive. Relieved that he did not seem to be involved in her death, Freeman quickly absolved himself from all blame.

On Thursday 17th November Constable Taylor was in the Anglesey Hotel asking questions about Catherine's whereabouts the previous Saturday night when Freeman approached him. He had been told that her corpse had been found that morning on Lees Common, and that her death probably occurred on the Saturday night because that was the last time she was seen alive. Freeman insisted that the police were wrong, and when asked why he was so sure, Freeman blurted out the tale Lunt had told Millington.

Police investigations soon uncovered Freeman, Platt and Fowler, as probable prime suspects in the crime and they were arrested by 20th November. With Freeman keeping to his story of James Lunt having seen Catherine Dooley alive on Sunday 15th November, the police had no option but to arrest Lunt.

Lunt had failed to see in his silly bragging that if Catherine had not died on the Saturday evening, then he might be implicated in her death. That only dawned on him when he stood in front of the bench of the Magistrates' Court with the others, accused of Catherine Dooley's murder.

THE
HEDNESFORD TRAGEDY

ANOTHER ARREST

The other three were soon implicated and sent down to await trial at Stafford Assizes. When it came to the case against Lunt, though, it soon became perfectly obvious that he had nothing at all to do with the murder. Edward Millington retold his account of the conversation in the blacksmith's shop and it was corroborated by William Wichnall, who had been present at the time. Both told the court that Lunt was prone to telling tall stories to appear popular, and they had never really believed him that morning.

Lunt was cross examined and confessed to making up the whole episode, but could offer no real explanation of why he had done so. His only connection with the attack was listening to Freeman's account as they walked to work on the Sunday. But could the court believe the new story if, as he had already confessed, he was such a liar? Might Lunt actually be responsible for allowing the old woman to die? This would not be murder, of course. And if he was totally innocent, what could the court do about him wasting valuable police time?

Deliberations by the bench were made in the full hearing of James Lunt, who squirmed with fear and embarrassment. Finally, Lord Hatherton, one of the Magistrates, addressed Lunt, telling him that he had only himself to blame for being himself accused of a terrible crime. He had "told a succession of falsehoods, right and left, but fortunately for Lunt, evidence was not enough to justify the Magistrates committing him for trial".

The Magistrates agreed that Lunt was aware that something dreadful was going on, but there was doubt as to whether he was aware what actually had happened, and they were going to give him the benefit of the doubt.

Lord Hatherton's remarks were obviously designed to frighten Lunt and teach him a lesson. Perhaps in future he might think twice before bragging to his friends. The shock treatment worked and it was a very relieved James Lunt who left the court with his friends.

On 8th March 1897, Freeman, Platt and Fowler appeared at Stafford Assizes charged with causing the death of Catherine Dooley. However, as the trial began, Mr Kettle, the Crown Prosecutor, said that he was prepared to offer no evidence against Platt, but wanted him called as a Prosecution witness against Fowler, and Platt was discharged.

Henry Freeman was also soon cleared of any wrongdoing. All the witnesses questioned swore that Freeman had nothing to do with the old lady being thrown over the hedge, nor had he gone into the field after her. Most agreed that he was simply helping her along the road in her drunken state. Two witnesses swore that Freeman had left the scene before any attack took place.

William Saunders was an errand boy from Chadsmoor who said that he saw Catherine thrown over the hedge, but that Freeman had remained in the road and done nothing. Instead, he had turned away and walked home with Saunders. As they were walking away William said that he had looked back and seen the other two men jump over the hedge.

A Mrs Bradbury, also of Chadmoor, said that she was returning from Hednesford that evening along the Cannock Road towards Less Common, when she heard a man say, "Let's throw the **** over the hedge". She was certain that it was neither Platt nor Freeman who uttered those words, but a third man. In fact, by the time she was thrown over Freeman had already left.

With no evidence to connect Freeman with either assault Mr Justice Wright instructed the jury to acquit him. Like Platt he was asked to give evidence in the remaining prosecution – that of John Fowler.

Fowler was the only person to be clearly named as an assailant. Not only had he been seen throwing Catherine over the hedge, but had gone into the field after her. What the jury had to decide was what happened there and whether Fowler intended to kill the old lady.

Catherine's body had evidence of bruising on the thighs, and witnesses spoke of hearing screams and shouts of "Don't kill me!" and a man saying, "Take that you old ***", but no one actually saw Fowler hitting the old woman. Even Platt could only say that "Fowler came up and pushed her on top of the hedge, saying that was the best place for such as her".

More witnesses said that later that evening, they spotted John Fowler running along the common land away from the direction in which the body was found. He had stopped and said to them, "Oh' don't tell them where I have gone". But was he running away from his victim who was dead? If so, why bother to say anything at all which might incriminate him?

The only clear evidence implicating Fowler in the attack was something overheard the following evening in the Jolly Collier Inn. Fowler was sitting with Platt when the latter turned and said, "What did you do with the old woman on Saturday night?" Fowler angrily replied, "Shut up, you **** fool, she's dead by now". Both Frederick Pritchard and George Bates swore that Fowler had uttered those exact words, "by now".

The difference in statements was not lost on the jury. If they believed Fowler had said "by now", it would mean that Catherine was still alive after his assault and he might be acquitted of murder.

Summing up, the judge pointed out that there were numerous witnesses who saw Fowler putting the woman over the hedge, and some who saw him climb after her, but there was no one who actually saw the attack. Although that was a cowardly act, in itself it had not killed her – she had died of exposure. Fowler was most certainly guilty of a crime, but not of murder. Accordingly, Mr Justice Wright instructed the jury to set aside the question of murder and decide whether Fowler was guilty of manslaughter.

When they returned the foreman of the jury announced their verdict of manslaughter. In sentencing Fowler the judge remarked, rather oddly, that he "thought the action of the Crown was right not to ask for a capital sentence though men had been hung on weaker evidence". Fowler was sentenced to three years penal servitude.

You may hope that today Fowler would have been facing a much stiffer sentence. In fact he might well have been convicted of the murder of Catherine Dooley. Nor would James Lunt have escaped with a telling off. He would have been charged with an offence which did not exist in 1896, that of wasting police time.

The Mysterious Marble
(Lichfield 1878 – Lichfield Mercury)

The 5th of November may summon up happy childhood memories of explosions, fountains of light in the sky and whirling demons of colour. You might also think of awesome bonfires and hot, sooty potatoes. On the other hand that date can bring to mind children blinded and burnt, and mobs throwing bricks at the fire brigade. Guy Fawkes Night in 1878 left some people with nothing but nightmares.

William George Green was landlord of the Gresley Arms Inn at Lichfield. Early that evening he and his lodgers were sitting in the pub kitchen listening to the crashes and reports of firework displays in the town. Perhaps they were reminiscing about boyhood bangers and bonfires. Tantalised and excited by the conversation, Green slipped away from the party and went next door to persuade young Henry Joseph Stych to lend him a pistol. Green was going to creep back in to the kitchen and fire the gun to frighten his lodgers.

Not knowing much about weapons, Green asked the young lad to prime the pistol for him. He stood and watched Stych charge the gun with powder and paper and, still excited, returned to the inn. Creeping along the passageway, he could hear the happy voices of the party in the kitchen.

As Green entered the room he must have stumbled and caught the gun on a freestanding partition separating the kitchen from the passage. The jolt caused it to fire and Samuel Bates collapsed.

In the pandemonium that followed, George Cotton, another lodger, looked at Bates and exclaimed, "Good God, he's shot!" In total disbelief, Green could only mumble, "There's nothing in the gun but powder, he cannot be hurt".

But a closer look showed blood pouring from Bates's skull. Sure that this was nothing but a dreadful accident, Green dispatched young Stych to find the doctor and the police superintendent.

When the two arrived they examined the body and Bates was pronounced dead. Because it seemed that the tragedy was purely accidental the Inquest was arranged for the following day. Meanwhile the surgeon would carry out his routine post mortem. However, what he found meant that the Inquest would not be a formality, for lodged in Bates's skull was a glass marble.

THE FATAL SHOOTING CASE AT
THE GRESLEY ARMS INN.

An inquest was held on Wednesday evening at the Gresley Arms Inn, before Mr. Charles Simpson, city coroner, on the body of Samuel Bates, labourer, of Walsall, who was shot dead on Tuesday night by William George Green, landlord of the above inn.

The following persons comprised the jury :—S. Pearsall (foreman,) W. Walmesley, Parton, Mason, Wright, Oakley, Simpson, J. Neeld, Hawkes, Nicholls, R. Smith, and Watkins.

An unusually stuffy announcement by the Mercury, even by the standards of 1878.

The Inquest began on the Wednesday morning under the local Coroner, Mr Simpson. Conveniently, it was held in the Gresley Arms Inn. The first to give evidence was young Henry Stych, who was so nervous that more than once the Coroner had to ask him to speak more loudly because the jury were finding it difficult to hear his evidence. Were those nerves brought on by the strain of the occasion or by some terrible guilty secret?

Stych said that he had been at home when Green arrived at about 8.00 pm on the evening of 5th November. The landlord had asked him for the loan of his gun, explaining that he wanted it to play a joke on the people at the inn. The gun was readily available, Stych told the court, as he had been using it that day for target practice.

Knowing that Green knew nothing about guns, he loaded it for him, but Stych was adamant that the landlord watched as he put in nothing but

54

powder and paper. When he had finished the two of them left the house at about 8.20 pm and went next door to the Gresley Arms.

Stych arrived in the kitchen first and sat down to watch the fun. When the gun fired he became confused because of the accident and the shouting. He told the jury that he thought that Green was near the fireplace when the gun fired, but could not be sure as he had his back to the screen. Green may have been behind him.

It was that uncertainty and Stych's nervous manner which led the jury to think that the lad might be hiding some information, and so they were allowed to question him more thoroughly. One juror, Mr Walmesley, asked about the marble found in Bates's skull, but the lad denied any knowledge of it and insisted vehemently that he did not put it in the gun, even as a prank. He added that he never saw Green put anything in the weapon either.

Still unsure of the lad's evidence, another juror called Mason asked Stych if he knew how the marble could have got into the muzzle of the gun. He even gave the lad an opportunity to absolve himself from blame by suggesting it may have been there accidentally. Stych refused to say anything that might implicate him in the death. He simply repeated that he had got the powder from a bottle and the paper from his pocket. He did admit that there had been bits of cork in his pocket, but he was certain there was no marble.

With the lad determined to argue his innocence, the Coroner dismissed him and called George Cotton. He was a bricklayer living at 41 Ball Street, Walsall who had come to work in Lichfield with Samuel Bates, James Ellson and Edward Plummer. They were all lodging at the Gresley Arms. After their day's work they had returned to the inn and were enjoying a chat in the kitchen when Green disappeared.

Cotton said that he was sitting by the fire while Bates stood with his back to the firegrate. Bates had stooped down to talk to him, possibly bringing his head below the top of the screen, when there was a loud explosion and Bates fell to the floor. Cotton saw blood coming from his mate's head and assumed he had been shot, though he never saw the gun.

He also told the jury that so far as he was concerned, Green had absolutely no motive for the shooting. In fact, he was sure that Green and Bates were very friendly, adding that Green was "sadly put about" at the accident.

The same evidence was given by both Edward Plummer and James Ellson. All three lodgers thought the shooting was purely accidental and the appearance of the marble was a total mystery. No one could offer any explanation as to how it got into the gun.

The next witness to take the stand was Mrs Stych. She had been standing in the doorway of the parlour when Green entered the pub. She noticed that he was carrying a gun and seemed to be creeping along the passageway. When he got near to the screen the muzzle of the weapon seemed to catch on an iron bar supporting the screen and it exploded, putting out the gaslight.

As Henry Stych's mother, she was asked by Mr Neeld, another juror, if she had ever seen marbles about her house. When she said that she was uncertain, Neeld thought she was being evasive and pressed for a more direct answer. When she remained unsure Neeld pressed further, but seeing her annoyance, Mr Simpson, the Coroner, intervened. Mrs Stych was then adamant that she had never seen any marbles.

Even so, Neeld felt that he was close to weakening her defences and continued to question her rather aggressively. Mrs Stych knew very well that he was trying to implicate her son in the death and became rude and awkward at his "silly" questions. Eventually the Coroner intervened again, saying that her statement was to be considered "not at all credible".

The last witness to the shooting was the unfortunate William Green, who was still in a state of shock. He told much the same story as the others. He had gone to Henry Stych's house to borrow the gun and asked the lad to prime it for him. He was sure that he had watched as the lad loaded it with half a charge of powder and some paper. Before he had taken the gun he had gone over to the fire and lit his pipe, but he could not swear if at any time he had his back to the boy.

When he left the house he had carried the gun under his right shoulder, supporting it with his right arm, thus making it "secure arms". He thought that it might have been slanting upwards. As he entered the pub he walked through the passage towards the kitchen, trying to remain undetected so as to surprise everyone. He could only suppose that the muzzle caught against the iron bar of the screen and then exploded.

When cross examined he said that as soon as Stych gave him the loaded gun, it never left his possession. He swore that he had put nothing into the muzzle because the powder and paper would be sufficient to cause the necessary noise for a 5thNovember prank. It was only when Cotton shouted that Bates was hurt that Green realised that something terrible had happened.

Green's gave his evidence in a subdued, straightforward way and the jury seemd to accept his story. But that still left them with the problem of how the marble got into the gun.

George William Homan was the surgeon called to the scene. He told the jury that he found Bates lying on the kitchen floor propped up by pillows. He was quite dead and had a wound on the left temple just above the eyebrow which was large enough to put a finger right into the brain. The post mortem revealed a marble embedded in the brain. At that point, Homan showed the object to the court, which caused cries of horror at its size.

From the direction of entry into the skull, Homan assessed that Bates had been bending down before the gun fired and had been hit as he was getting up again. That confirmed Cotton's account.

As the surgeon's evidence told them little more than they already knew, the jury asked to be shown the pub's kitchen where the shooting had taken place. Here they asked to be shown peoples' positions when the gun exploded and for a clearer explanation of how the gun was primed.

Having seen the room, and with Green having explained his movements again in precise detail, the jury seemed satisfied with his account. When they returned to the temporary courtroom they asked for young Henry Stych to be recalled and he was re-examined about the marble.

It seemed that the jury were more than prepared to accept that the object got into the weapon without anyone knowing. Mr Neeld suggested that they look at the powder bottle in case the marble had been inside, but it was too big to go in.

The jury suggested that perhaps Stych did not know the marble was there? Had he been using marbles for his target practice and accidentally left one in the gun? Despite their obvious attempts to give the lad avenues of escape, Stych was determined to deny all knowledge of the object. Eventually, the Coroner dismissed him and concluded the Inquest.

In his summing up Mr Simpson said that Green had been doing nothing unlawful when the gun exploded. Everybody in the pub was on friendly terms and there had been no suggestion of any disturbance. If the jury were satisfied that the gun fired accidentally, then the ordinary verdict of accidental death should be their judgement.

It was here that Mr Neeld intervened. Still convinced that young Stych had placed the marble in the weapon he asked, "Supposing it could be proved that the lad did put the marble in the gun?" What, he wanted to know, should be their verdict then? To which Mr Simpson replied, "Then I do not know that it would make the least difference." That brought a quick retort from Mr Oakley, another juror, who commented, "At least it would clear up the mystery."

But the mystery was never solved. The jury returned a verdict of accidental death while still seeming to believe that Henry Joseph Stych knew more than he admitted about the fatal marble.

The Strange Confession of Henry Sides
(Newcastle 1887 – Staffs Sentinel)

On the afternoon of Sunday 2nd December 1887, Sergeant Maudley was on patrol in Red Lion Square, Newcastle. At 10 minutes to 4 he was approached by Henry Sides who asked for directions to the nearest police station. The man seemed very nervous so Sergeant Maudley asked him why he needed the police. All that Sides would tell him was that he wanted to give himself up for a "very bad crime".

Unable to extract more than this, the sergeant took Sides to Newcastle Police Station and got the help of Sergeant Bentley. The two officers interviewed Sides and Bentley took down the following statement.

> "I am a clerk and was formerly in the employ of Lord Hereford at Prycoal. [possibly Prygol] On the 23rd or 24th November 1886, Margaret Bowen, a domestic servant, came to see me. I kept company with her. I took her a walk to Penmase Farm, [Penmaes] kept by Mrs Vaughan at Llanfillo, Brecon. [Llanfilo] About ten o'clock, I gave her a bottle and asked her to drink. It contained port wine. I had mixed some laudanum and other drug with it.
>
> After she had drunk it, she became ill and lay down on the grass in the orchard, and she died within a few minutes. I then took her body to the hedge side and left it there until about one o'clock the next morning. I returned there and dug a hole, and buried the body at the back of the barn. I found some lime in the garden, which I put on her before I put the turf on. It took me until about four a.m. to dig the hole and bury her."

Dumbfounded by this ample confession, the sergeants were puzzled as to why the man had not confessed before, or why the police in Wales had not circulated information about the missing woman. Having got Sides to sign the confession in a "cramped and unsteady hand", they questioned him further. He said he had been wandering all over the place since he had done the murder, but could not settle because it grieved him so much. In the end he decided to give himself up and had walked that morning from Nantwich to do so.

Perhaps sensing that the two officers did not believe his story, Sides offered to take them to the exact spot where he had buried his victim. It was that offer that forced them to keep him in custody, although both men doubted Sides' sanity. Despite their scepticism though, they decided to set further investigations in motion.

Under the supervision of the Chief Constable, Mr Datton, Sides's details were sent to the Brecon Police at Llanfilo. Sides was 27 years old and had lived in Wales for most of his life. He was about 5ft 7ins tall and rather strongly built. Most likely he had worked as a farm labourer for most of his life.

THE EXTRAORDINARY CONFESSION OF MURDER AT NEWCASTLE.

How do you think the Sentinel would handle it today?

FRUITLESS SEARCH FOR THE BODY.

All that the Newcastle police could do was to wait for information but keep Sides in custody in case his story was true. For this they needed approval from the magistrates' court, so on the following Monday morning at 11 am he was taken before the Borough Police Court.

Dressed in shabby corduroy trousers and a light coloured jacket and with a running sore on his left ear, which he ascribed to a constant cold, Sides looked a sorry sight. He was clearly troubled, which could be seen from the "restless and furtive appearance" of his face and eyes. But was it from the knowledge that he had murdered Margaret Bowen or a sign of mental instability?

The evidence at hand seemed to suggest the latter. Chief Constable Datton told the Magistrates that he had looked up all available police documents on outstanding crimes in the Brecon area and further afield, but could find no record of any crime committed in that part of Wales. He told the court he thought "there is nothing in it [Sides' confession] at all". The Magistrates agreed, but to be on the safe side they preferred to remand the prisoner for another week to await the outcome of investigations in Wales.

The reports did not take long. By the morning of Thursday 6th December the Chief Constable had a letter from Superintendent Flye of the Brecon Police. Acting on the confession he had taken his officers to Penmaes Farm where they had dug up the area around the barn near the orchard, but found nothing.

Mrs Vaughan, owner of the farm, confirmed that Henry Sides had worked there during the latter part of 1886, and at the same time, Margaret Bowen had been employed as a domestic servant. However, the girl had left her job at Penmaes on the first Tuesday of November 1886, and so far as Mrs Vaughan knew, she was living nearby perfectly alive and well.

The Brecon Police had managed to track down Margaret Bowen. She was living under the name of Margaret Jones, and to prove her identity showed them an recent Order of Affiliation granting her the care of a child.

Superintendent Flye could have stopped his investigations there, but he was intrigued by the affair and delved further into the character of Henry Sides. His second report made interesting but disturbing reading.

After leaving work at Penmaes Farm, Sides had persuaded a grocer in Brecon to lend him some money on the strength of what appeared to be a warrant for deferred army pay. Others in the area had advanced cash to Sides on the same document, which proved to be false. Those questioned thought that Sides suffered from a "slight defect of intellect", but were equally sure that he was endowed with "plenty of cunning, craft and untruth".

Further investigations showed that Sides was nothing more than a liar, or at best a romancer. The police at Llangollen, Denbighshire, reported that a man answering the description of Sides had wanted to give himself up less than two months ago in September 1887, (note the date) claiming that he was a patient who had escaped from Shrewsbury lunatic asylum. However, noting his healthy condition and 'knowing' that he lived in the Oswestry area, they had refused to lock him up. Strangely, this turned out to be the only thing Sides said which was not fantasy.

The authorities at Hay in Breconshire reported that Sides had worked at Tymawr, Llanigon, for about two weeks in June 1886. At the end of May 1887 he had told them that he was to meet the local peer, for whom he had once worked, in the hope of getting another job. Having checked with that peer, Sides' story proved nothing more than another series of inventions.

The final and conclusive information received by Chief Constable Datton was from Mr Arthur Strange, medical superintendent of the asylum at Bicton Heath, near Shrewsbury. A man answering Sides's description had been admitted to his asylum from Oswestry as a 'lunatic' in October 1886. He had escaped on 1st June 1887, but as he had not been retaken within the statutory limit of fourteen days, he had been entered in their register as discharged. At the time of his escape he was deemed 'insane'.

The Newcastle police had all the information they needed. Henry Sides was not a murderer. He was just one of those unfortunates who, for whatever reason, seemed compelled to accuse themselves of horrific crimes. What was to become of Henry Sides was of little concern to the Newcastle police – they were just glad that their mystery had been solved.

Provoking Henry Myatt
(Newcastle 1895 – Staffs Sentinel)

Henry Myatt lived with his wife and daughter at 5 Holborn, Newcastle. For most of his working life he was a miner, but shortly before the incident he had given up pit work and taken to selling fish for a living. Did Myatt becoming an independent trader make his neighbours envious?

On the evening of Sunday 16th June 1895 he arrived home after a long day's work to be met at his door by Martin Leech junior, who lived next door at number 7. Leech was obviously the worse for drink and demanded that Myatt sell him some fish. Not wanting a scene, Myatt asked Leech to wait outside while he got him the fish. For some reason, Leech took exception to that and demanded to be allowed inside. Myatt refused to let him in and Leech began to swear loudly.

Still not wanting a row, Myatt tried to take Leech home. Three times Myatt tried and each time Leech became more abusive, finally insulting Myatt's wife and daughter who had come outside to see what the noise was about.

Their appearance seemed to have incensed Leech all the more, and he insisted that he fight Myatt. Annoyed at the drunk's behaviour, Myatt squared up to him and managed to strike the first blow. Although not a powerful punch, it took Leech off his feet and he fell backwards, banged his head on the road and passed out.

The commotion had brought Martin Leech senior from his bed, and seeing his son lying in the street he shouted that Myatt had killed his boy. With the help of a passing stranger he got his son inside number 7 and laid him on the sofa. It was not until the following morning (Monday) that he called a doctor and Martin Leech junior was taken to the local workhouse, but he never regained consciousness.

At 5.15 p.m. on the Monday afternoon, Henry Myatt was interviewed by Sergeant Bentley at the Plough Inn. Shortly after he was taken to the police station and charged with causing the death of Martin Leech.

The various court hearings that followed where all concerned with the weight of Myatt's blow and whether he struck Leech intending to do him physical harm or just to defend himself.

At the initial Borough Police Court [magistrates] hearing held on Tuesday 17th June, Myatt admitted to hitting Leech in self defence, but only after a great deal of provocation. He said that he had only taken Leech by the arm to guide him home, but the third time he tried Leech had broken free and demanded a fight. During the row he had pushed Leech, who had fallen over and hit his head on the roadway. Myatt then took his family back into number 5 and knew nothing of Leech's fate until the police saw him at the Plough Inn.

Martin Leech senior's version of the disturbance was rather different. He said that he had been woken up by the row and when he got outside, Myatt was in his shirtsleeves standing near his son, who was lying on the broad of his back on the ground. The young man's eyes were closed and he could not speak. It was then that he had accused Myatt of killing his son.

Questioned by the magistrates, Leech insisted that he had seen his son fall after Myatt hit him, but when questioned more closely he said that Myatt had "pushed" his son. He was told to be careful of what he said, and quickly changed to saying Myatt had "knocked him down". Accused then of changing his mind too often, Leech insisted that he had seen Myatt hit his son.

When the Coroner's Court sat on the Wednesday 18th June, Leech senior had changed his story again. To the Inquest he admitted that in fact he had never seen any blow struck as it was all over by the time he got outside number 7. So what exactly, the Coroner asked, did happen in the "fight" between Leech and Myatt?

Patrick Rourke was a 14 year old lad who lived at the Blue Bull Yard. He told the court that at about a 10.15 on the Sunday evening he saw Leech junior and Mrs Myatt and her daughter standing in the street outside number 5, Holborn. Leech was swearing at Miss Myatt while Mr Myatt was trying to persuade him to go home. Then Myatt said that he "could not stand it any longer" and pushed the deceased, who fell down and cut his face.

Angry now, Leech had got up and gone into the middle of the road, where he took off his jacket and "offered Myatt out to fight". Myatt went towards him and Martin Leech rushed at him. In the attempt to stop his attacker Myatt "hit him a slight blow on the chest". Leech fell backwards, catching his head on the road as he landed. He did not get up.

When Martin Leech senior came out he shouted at Myatt and the prisoner replied, "I'd swing for a man like him". Myatt then went back into his home and Leech junior was carried into No 7 by Leech and a man named Walklate. Questioned by the Coroner, young Rourke said that Leech junior was "drunk, noisy and rowing", but admitted that Leech had not struck Myatt before the blow felled him.

Another young lad, 15 year old John Moran, had also been attracted to the scene by the noise and told much the same story. He had arrived just in time to see Myatt strike Leech, who fell flat on his back and lay quite still.

Sergeant Bentley gave evidence that when he heard about the "fight" he had been called to the Leech household at 1 o'clock on the Monday afternoon. When he saw the state of Leech junior he had him taken to the workhouse where Leech died at 4 o'clock. At that point the Sergeant searched out Henry Myatt and arrested him for causing the death of the deceased.

The final witness was Mr R H Dickson, the surgeon who had performed the post mortem. He said that he had first been called to 7 Holborn at 10 o'clock on the Monday morning. Leech junior was unconscious and suffering from a lacerated wound to the back of his head. He had probed the wound but could find no evidence of a skull fracture. Convinced that his patient was not in any immediate danger, he had left.

At the post mortem, though, he found that the skull had been fractured and that Leech had died from compression of the brain due to a large blood clot. When asked if the delay in treating the deceased might have caused the death, Mr Dickson said that in his opinion, "the injuries were so severe that nothing could have saved him".

The Coroner summed up the case for the jury, remarking that it was not their duty to find the prisoner guilty or not of the crime, but added that "unless the death was the result of an accident, or that Myatt was bound to do what he did in self-defence, then he was guilty of manslaughter" and should be tried.

The jury indicted Myatt for manslaughter, adding that he had been under "great provocation". Myatt was committed for trial but released on bail of £50 with two sureties of £25 each.

When the Borough Police Court sat again on Thursday 20th June, Mr Sproston, Myatt's solicitor, argued that to try his client would be a waste of taxpayers' money because the Assizes would clearly dismiss the case. He acknowledged that his client had struck a blow, but the "push" was not sufficient in itself to cause Leech to fall and hit his head. It was because the deceased was drunk that he toppled over. "Pushing was not manslaughter", and that was all that his client had done. Had not every man the right to defend himself and his family? Leech's death was nothing more than a tragic accident. However, should the court still wish Leech to be prosecuted then their only charge should be one of "justifiable homicide". [Odd this, because there is no such offence.]

Unfortunately for Mr Sproston, the magistrates did not agree and Henry Myatt was remanded to await trial in Stafford on the charge of manslaughter.

The trial began on 26th July 1895 and it soon became clear that Mr Sproston's prediction was correct. After the evidence of young Patrick Rourke, who confirmed that the "push was not a violent one, nor was the blow", Mr Boddam, defending Myatt, asked Mr Justice Hawkins if the trial need go any further.

After a brief deliberation, the judge pointed out to Mr Fisher, Counsel for the prosecution, that the evidence presented before the court "clearly showed that the deceased had brought upon himself his death entirely by his own misbehaviour". Naturally, when the prisoner heard Leech swearing at his daughter he had remonstrated. Leech ran at him and Myatt was only acting within his lawful rights in keeping Leech off. The consequence of the push appeared to be "entirely accidental".

The judge added that unless the prosecution could produce evidence to show that Myatt had not acted purely in self-defence, and with as much restraint as was humanly possible, then he should end the trial. As there was no further evidence, the jury retired and within minutes returned with a verdict of not guilty. Henry Myatt was acquitted of manslaughter and the minor charge of assault, and walked free from the court.

"Not come by fair means.."
(Penkridge 1856 – Staffs Advertiser)

At the end of the summer of 1855, twenty three year old Martha Guest had left her home in Penkridge to work at a pub in Wolverhampton. It was run by an unmarried man called Derry, and it did not take him long to get her pregnant. Just six weeks before Christmas she left the pub to be confined in a house owned by one Thomas Whittal, a good friend of Derry. Here she was cared for by Hannah Dyer, Whittal's mistress, until she gave birth to a baby girl on 17th February 1856.

Three weeks later Martha's mother, Elizabeth Guest, arrived to collect the child and take her back to Penkridge where she "dry nursed" the infant. Martha remained at the Whittal household for another week and then went to her mother's home.

All seemed well until 3rd May when Martha took the baby to Mr Mackenzie, a Penkridge surgeon. He diagnosed the child to be well, except that it could have done with some mother's milk, and he just prescribed some powders to help its digestion.

By 9th May though, Martha had sent for Mrs Saunders, a surgeon's widow renowned locally for being good with the rearing of sickly children. Not considering the infant to be in any real danger, she said that magnesia powders would help the child and left thinking that all would be well. On 13th May she was summoned again but still thought nothing was wrong. On 14th May infant Mary Elizabeth Derry died and she was buried on 16th May.

People assumed this was just the tragic death of a sickly infant in an age when such deaths were common. That was until Thomas Whittal entered the scene again, offering the view that there was something suspicious in the child's death and the Guests' behaviour in the days surrounding the mishap.

Police investigations and the Inquest led to the indictment and arrest of Elizabeth and Martha Guest on charges of murdering the infant. On 23rd July 1856 their trial began at the Stafford Assizes under Mr Justice Wightman.

The first witness was Hannah Dyer, who freely admitted that she was Whittal's mistress and that they had lived together for years. Most of the time they had lived in Wolverhampton, but at the time of the trial they were living in Cannock. Six weeks before Christmas 1855 Martha Guest had come to stay with them in Wolverhampton during the latter stages of her pregnancy. When the baby was born in the February, she appeared healthy and remained with Hannah for three weeks and three days. During that time there was never any sign that the child was anything but perfectly well.

A.TEW

66

After mother and child had left for Penkridge Hannah heard no more of them until the Saturday before Whit Monday (10th May), when she met Elizabeth Guest in Wolverhampton's market place. Asking after the baby, Hannah was upset to hear that the child was "rather poorly".

When she asked why she and Whittal had not been told, Hannah was worried by Elizabeth's reply. "I did not send you word because Whittal might think I had done something to the child, because I have had the money." Confused, Hannah asked which money this was, and Elizabeth said that Martha had received £20 from Derry to help with the child's upkeep. Hannah told the courts that she was mystified when Elizabeth mentioned the money because it was not hers or Whittal's business what money Derry gave to the child's mother.

Elizabeth's defensive tone concerned Hannah and she offered to visit the Guests in Penkridge. However, Elizabeth said there would be no need because Martha would go to the Whittals's home on Monday 12th to collect Hannah and take her to see the baby.

When Monday arrived, Martha did visit Hannah and was accompanied by her younger sister, but instead of returning to Penkridge with Hannah, she promised to write should the baby become worse. She did write, but the letter did not arrive until Saturday 17th May and it announced that Martha had gone to Liverpool with the child. [The letter later proved to have been written by Elizabeth]. This made Whittal very anxious about the child's welfare, and he decided to visit Penkridge himself.

As the court heard later when he gave evidence, Whittal started to walk to Penkridge from Cannock on 19th May, but on the way was surprised to meet both mother and daughter. Remarking that he thought Martha was in Liverpool, Martha told him that he must have been mistaken as it was her sister, Betsy, who had taken the child there. Back home he started to worry about the child's whereabouts and asked Hannah if she would visit the Guests the following day.

Hannah set off on 20th May and when she arrived at the village she inquired after the Guests' cottage, only to be told by a villager that the child had died.

For some reason she did not tell Elizabeth that she knew the awful news, and was astounded when Elizabeth told her that the baby was still in Liverpool. Even more devastating was Martha's announcement that she had received two letters declaring that baby Mary was, "a little better".

Eventually, when Martha was alone with Hannah, she admitted that the child was dead. Her reasons for acting so strangely were because the death of the child had left her extremely depressed. She had wanted to tell Whittal and even wanted him to make a coffin, but her mother had advised her against it. Finally she told Hannah that the surgeon, Mr Mackenzie, had said that death was due to a "watery head".

As Hannah was about to leave, Martha asked her if she would get Whittal to write to Derry and ask him for a further £10 as her mother had kept the first £20. She also promised to visit Whittal as soon as possible to explain the baby's death more fully.

Hannah told the court that when she returned home that evening Whittal was very concerned. He immediately wrote to the Guests saying that he was highly suspicious that the child's death was "not come by fair means", and unless he was satisfied he would institute an inquiry. He also said that he would write to Derry about his suspicions. The letter brought no response.

By 11th June Whittal had written again, and that letter brought Martha to his home. When she arrived there was little to show that she might be frightened at his threats. Instead she was extremely angry and began shouting at Whittal. Hannah clearly remembered Martha saying, "You don't think I've poisoned it? It doesn't matter to you if I have." She also told him that she had shown his letter to a Mr Lister, a surgeon, and he had told her that Whittal was trying to extort money and she was to ignore his threats.

Martha added that the child was nothing to do with Whittal and if he tried to investigate further she would make him suffer, especially if the body were exhumed. She implied that she would bankrupt him as she could "find money longer than he could". With that threat, Martha had left. Whittal was so angry at being accused of blackmail that he went to the police. Hannah's last piece of evidence concerned a time before the child had been born. Five or six weeks before the birth Martha had told Hannah that she would not mind making away with the child. When cross examined Hannah insisted that the statement meant killing the infant, not going to Liverpool.

Whittal's testimony added little more to the case than Hannah's evidence but he was to undergo severe questioning by Mr Huddleston, for the defence. He tactic was to blacken Whittal's character.

Whittal was a carpenter and joiner by trade, but Huddleston accused him of wanting to be a "fortune teller" (notorious as gossips and liars) and that he had even practised it. Whittal denied this, almost laughing. He had told fortunes, he said, but only as party games like many people did.

Huddleston next asked about Whittal's relationship with Hannah Dyer, hoping to prove that Whittal was of low moral character by the polite standards of the time. Whittal freely admitted that they lived outside marriage, but his real wife still lived in Wolverhampton and had not been with him for twenty years. More important, she knew about Hannah and did not care.

Asked why, if he was "acting in the interests of society", it had taken him from 24th May to 11th June before telling the police, Whittal simply replied that he had wanted to allow the Guests time to explain their actions. When Huddleston implied that Whittal had hoped to blackmail the women, he vehemently denied it.

Finally, Huddleston questioned Whittal's honesty. Why had he said that he had written to Derry when clearly he had not? And why had he told Hannah Dyer that he had left papers at the Guests' home? Whittal's said that these were purely methods of trying to force the Guests into telling him more about the child's situation. If they knew Derry had become involved and Hannah visited their cottage, then they would have to be more forthcoming.

The more Huddleston questioned Whittal, the more plausible he appeared, and so eventually he was allowed to leave the stand and the next witness was called.

Mrs Margaret Saunders was the widow of a much respected surgeon who was called to see the child some days before it died. Thinking the baby to be costive or constipated, she prescribed a mixture of magnesia and rhubarb. On her next visit she took more of the mixture, but the child was much worse. She was concerned that while Elizabeth nursed the infant it kept moving its head.

When she returned to the Guests' home on the following day (14th May) the child was dead. Both mother and grandmother told her that the cause was "water on the head", but she had not asked them how they knew. Under cross examination Mrs Saunders said that at no time was she told of bruising on the back of the child's head. Whenever she visited the baby was always wearing a bonnet.

The next witness was Nancy Roberts, a neighbour of the Guests. She told the court that the family were kind to the child, despite having four other girls in the house. Even so, Mrs Roberts could not remember any of them telling her of the child's head injury, which seemed curious because they usually mentioned family illnesses.

What was the head injury that witnesses were being asked about? At the Inquest the Coroner had ordered an exhumation and post mortem which was carried out by two surgeons who now gave evidence at the trial. By coincidence, one of them had seen the baby shortly before she died.

Mr Mackenzie first saw the baby on 3rd May. He felt that there was nothing really the matter and he had prescribed a powder of mercury and chalk. When the mother appeared again the next day, he surmised that she was overwrought and reassured her by saying that the child was well and only needed good nursing and mother's milk.

He had not seen Martha Guest until 14th May when she appeared asking him to certify the cause of death. He had refused because he was not certain how the child had died. Martha told him that she had died from water on the brain, which she insisted that he had diagnosed. He denied ever saying such a thing and swore as much in court.

Mr Mackenzie said that at the post mortem he and Mr Lister had discovered traces of antimony in the stomach and liver, though not enough to cause death or even sickness. More important than this metallic element, though, was a considerable bruise on the back of the head that had penetrated through to the skull. A blood clot had formed and caused the death. It was "such as would be caused by considerable violence – a blow, or a fall, or some hard substance which would cause it".

Mr Lister, was both a surgeon and the Penkridge Registrar of Births, Marriages and Deaths. He agreed with Mackenzie's evidence, stating that the injury "must have required considerable violence to inflict". Was Lister suggesting that he thought the injury was by human hands? It looked like it. But the rest of his evidence was more alarming.

On 16th May Elizabeth Guest had arrived at his office asking him to register the infant's death. He had refused because no doctor had seen the child immediately before it died. Elizabeth then told him that Mr Mackenzie had seen the baby nine or ten days before and said that she was suffering from dropsy, which finally caused death. On the strength of this Lister reluctantly issued the certificate, registering the child in the name of Derry.

When Lister was asked about his conversation with Martha concerning Whittal's letter and his advice to her about blackmail, he was astounded. He had never had such a conversation and most certainly had never seen any letter. In fact Mr Lister was certain that he had never seen Martha in connection with the child or Whittal.

Suspicions against the two women seemed to be mounting up, but at this point in the trial Mr Justice Wightman intervened. He asked the jury if the defence needed to call the prisoners to the witness box. "No direct evidence" had been produced by the prosecution "as to the person who caused the injury". Mr Mackenzie, the surgeon, had admitted that the injury "might have been caused by a fall", and there was no evidence to show that the blow to the head was not accidental. Whatever suspicions might exist, the prosecution had not made out their case of murder beyond reasonable doubt.

The judge added "it appears that there was no motive for the crime, as Mr Derry was prepared to pay more money when it was needed". Having listened carefully to the judge's comments the jury acquitted both women, adding that in their view no crime had been committed.

Whittal must have left the courtroom with grave doubts. If the child's injury was accidental, why did the women tell so many lies? Why all the elaborate cover stories and the threats to Whittal if they were innocent? And why was Martha Guest so afraid of the exhumation?

The Body in Shaft 7
(Silverdale 1875 – Staffs Sentinel)

The longer a crime is unsolved, the greater the chance that it will remain so. But what chance do the police have if nothing is ever reported because relatives are not sure that a crime has been committed?

For several weeks in mid 1875 miners at the Rompin Colliery had been complaining of a lack of air in one of the galleries. Thinking that one of the airshafts might be blocked, the manager sent Enoch Dale and a group of colliers to investigate. What they discovered was gruesome. Lodged in the scaffold of the shaft was the decomposed body of a man lying on its side.

The corpse was covered in soot but quite naked but for a piece of rag around one arm. That arm, though, was separated from the rest of the body and lay close to one leg. The body was badly decayed so the men had great difficulty getting it out of the shaft. When they succeeded it was taken to the local mortuary to be seen by Mr Ralph Goodall, a surgeon from Silverdale.

At the first sitting of the Coroner's Inquest on 10th June, Mr Goodall reported that "the whole body seemed to be mutilated and the leg was broken. The skull was entire, but was partially removed". However, as the corpse was almost unrecognisable he could not say whether the injuries were inflicted before death or not, but felt that the arm had been cut from the

71

body before it fell down the shaft. The shaft was 140 yards deep and the arm could have been knocked off during the fall, but Mr Goodall doubted it.

A.TEW

The only other witness questioned at the first hearing was Samuel Sharratt, a collier from Finney Green. He told the court that he was the brother in law of the dead man, one Cain Lawton. He had gone to the mortuary to look at the body because his brother in law had been missing since December 1874. He had recognised the body because of the clothing found with it. The boots and the trousers were Cain's, and some other boots found nearby had been those purchased by his own wife at Newcastle, in the December, which she had asked Cain Lawton to carry home for her.

Sharratt had last seen his brother in law on the evening of 19th December at Newcastle when he left him in a pub between 9 and 10 o'clock with a friend called Joseph Brindley. Lawton would have left with him because he lodged with Sharratt, but he stayed to have another drink with Brindley.

The Coroner asked why the family had not reported the missing relative. Samuel said they assumed that he had gone to work elsewhere as a butty miner, that is, a freelance who moved around the district from mine to mine. As to Cain Lawton's state of mind, Sharratt said that he had known the deceased for seventeen years and he had never seemed affected in his mind. So far as Sharratt was concerned, he was a happily married man who never drank too much and had no enemies.

He did tell the Inquest that he had heard his brother in law had been in some sort of skirmish with men in Church Street, but he had not seen it, just been told of it. The Coroner interrupted him, reminding him that the court could not deal in gossip, but that it was worth investigation.

At that point he adjourned the hearing, adding that it was for the police to ascertain whether Cain Lawton had met his death by accident or foul play. All he would say at that time was "at present, the circumstances were anything but satisfactory", and he hoped the police might have further evidence before the next Inquest hearing.

Before that happened gossip spread quickly. Silverdale was a small community and news of the terrible find at the local pit travelled fast. Stories began to surface about Cain Lawton's last movements, and in particular concerning a fight between Lawton and two men, William Luke and John Ratcliffe. Rumour had it that both had bragged about having seen to it that Lawton would not bother them again. The police were quick to act and both men were arrested. Ratcliffe was still in the area but Luke had left and was found at Littleborough, near Rochdale.

When the inquest resumed at the Sneyd Arms Inn, Mr Booth, the Coroner, had much to find out. What had caused Lawton's death. Was he alive or dead when he fell down the shaft? Could he have committed suicide? Was his fall the result of a fight at the head of the shaft? Was Cain Lawton's fall down the shaft clearly accidental or was there was sufficient evidence to send Luke and Ratcliffe for trial for murder?

The position and state of the corpse in the shaft might clarify matters, so the first witnesses to be called were men present when the body was found.

Enoch Dale told the court that they had great difficulty in extricating the corpse from the shaft because it was so badly decomposed. However, when it had been removed they found a boot nearby, one stocking and a pair of trousers. The trousers were found on the top scaffold and in the pocket was £1.1s 11d. [about £1.10p] The pockets did not seem to have been rifled.

John Whitmore, colliery engineman, testified that he had been called to the scene after the body was found. The corpse was on the scaffold, some 15 yards from the pit bottom and the left arm lay away from the body. At this stage they had not moved the corpse. However, as they lifted the body from the scaffold part of the head came away.

Whitmore told the hearing that he had later been allocated the job of searching the shaft and had come across a jacket hanging from one of the scaffold beams, some 12 yards from where they found the body. He had also found a shirt and a singlet, again feet from where the body lay. Further searching uncovered a pair of women's boots.

Joseph Whitmore was an engineman from Scott Hay and brother of the last witness. On the Sunday before Christmas Day 1874 he had passed the shaft of No. 7, the Rompin Colliery, at about 10.30 in the morning. About 20 yards from the mouth of the shaft he had found a hat which was later identified as Cain Lawton's.

There was some snow on the ground, but it was unscuffed and smooth and showed no signs of a struggle having taken place near the shaft. To keep people away from the shaft there was fencing around it and iron plates lay half way over the hole. Although there was a track nearby which was well used, "it was scarcely likely that a man could stumble over the fence into the pit". He had examined the area around but found no traces of blood or the "slightest indication that a deadly murder had taken place".

James Lucas, colliery manager, described the layout of the pit. The shaft, he said, was about 80 yards from the main road and was fenced with railings 3 feet high, which were quite sufficient to keep any person from stumbling down it by accident. Besides that, there were plates over the hole.

Asked how he thought the body might come to be down the shaft, Lucas said that in his opinion, the corpse was naked before it was put into the shaft and the clothes thrown down afterwards.

If the jury were still in doubt as to whether Cain Lawton committed suicide or not, the Coroner recalled the surgeon, Mr Goodall. He repeated his previous evidence, but when asked if he could be sure that the deceased was dead before he went down the shaft he had to say that, "it was impossible to say if the body went down the pithead dead or alive" due to its decomposition. He knew that some men, when in drink, had delirium tremens and strange hallucinations and often jumped from windows. At such times they had suicidal intentions, but he never knew of a case where a man had stripped off his clothes before jumping.

The surgeon's evidence convinced the jury that they were not dealing with suicide, but was Lawton dead or alive when he went down the shaft? And they had still heard no evidence to implicate anyone in his death.

Joseph Brindley gave evidence next. He was a butty collier like Cain Lawton, and on the evening of 19th December he was with him in the Black Horse at Newcastle until about 11 o'clock. They left together and went to Church Street where they entered the house of James Lloyd. There they lit their pipes and chatted, and when they came out they met two men, one of them being John Ratcliffe whom Brindley recognised.

Words were exchanged between the two men and Lawton, then the second man, not Ratcliffe, struck Lawton and knocked him down. The witness picked Lawton up and tried to stop the quarrel, but Ratcliffe took off his coat and tried to continue the fight. However, Lawton would not fight and walked away towards New Town, saying that he would not go home that night but stay in Silverdale. That was the last time Brindley saw Lawton alive.

Responding to a question from the jury, Brindley said that the men hit Lawton for no reason. As he went down a bottle of rum fell out of his pocket, and the two men picked it up and started to drink it. Lawton had not tried to retrieve it but simply walked away. The witness had left the two men drinking the rum and had gone home to Madeley. He arrived there at about 2 o'clock on the Sunday morning.

On the Tuesday morning, 22nd December, Brindley saw Ratcliffe again and something was said about the rum drinking. He also told Ratcliffe that Lawton was missing, to which Ratcliffe replied that Lawton was probably off drinking somewhere. On the following Sunday he went with Samuel Sharratt to see Ratcliffe. At first, Ratcliffe refused to identify the man who had been with him on the Saturday, but being pressed, he said that it had been William Luke.

Next called to give evidence was Philip James, a miner living in Church Street, Silverdale. He told the hearing that he had seen Lawton, Brindley, William Luke and John Ratcliffe just after midnight on 19th December. They were quarrelling and Luke had struck Lawton, who fell. James went into his house at this point but came out again later to see if the men had gone. This time he saw Ratcliffe with his coat on challenging Lawton to fight. Lawton refused and walked away down the street. The men had followed him a short distance behind and Brindley came and spoke to James. When he last saw the three men they were going into Isaac Rowley's house.

Ephraim Mountford lodged with Philip James. He had seen everything that James had told the hearing, but added that Ratcliffe had said to Lawton as he lay on the ground, "I'll be your ***** butcher".

Richard Dodd also lived in Church Street. He had gone to bed around 12 o'clock that night but before he went to sleep he had been roused by someone "scrattling" [quarrelling]. He had heard cries of "Murder" two or three times, but had not got up as "it was a very frequent thing to have rows at night in Silverdale"

With evidence mounting against the two prisoners and many more witnesses to hear, Mr Booth adjourned the Inquest until the next day. By that time word had got around Silverdale and other parts of the Potteries so that when the Inquest reopened a large crowd gathered. Ratcliffe, for his part, seemed totally unperturbed by the whole affair, even smiling to the crowd.

First witness to be called on the second day was Emma Rowley, wife of Isaac Rowley and a relation to Cain Lawton's wife. She told the court that on 20th December she had gone down to James Edwards's house in Church Street to see if her husband was there. Between half past 2 and 3 o'clock in the afternoon, Ratcliffe and Luke came into the house. Ratcliffe said that he and Luke had had a scuffle with Cain Lawton and "he knew that the ***** would carry black flesh". Isaac Rowley warned Ratcliffe to be careful what he said as Emma was related to Mrs Lawton. After that Ratcliffe said no more and left about 5 o'clock, while Luke stayed until about 10.

Eliza Edwards, wife of James Edwards, said that Ratcliffe and Luke had been at her home in the early hours of 20th December and had stayed until about 4 o'clock in the morning. They were "like men who had had a drop of drink" and were singing and playing the harmonium.

[So it seems that Ratcliffe and Luke were at Edwards's house both in the early hours of 20th December till 4.00 am (Eliza Edwards), and returned there at between 2 and 3.00 pm (Emma Rowley). We dared to wonder whether the *Sentinel's* reporter or typesetter might have confused am and pm, and that both women were really referring to the early hours. But whilst Eliza and Emma might have been referring to approximately the same times for R and L's arrival, (Eliza – "early hours", Emma – "2/3 o'clock"), it is difficult to reconcile the times of leaving, (Eliza –"about 4am", Emma – R until 5am and L until 10.]

A member of the jury, possibly thinking the early visit the more significant, asked if either Ratcliffe or Luke were bloody. Eliza said that neither was and they had not asked for soap or water to wash themselves. They certainly did not look as if they had just murdered someone. Her husband, James, confirmed that fact, adding that their conversation was of "an ordinary character".

However, Isaac Rowley, who was also present at the Edwards' house that evening, said that when Luke and Ratcliffe came in they said that they had had a "falling out" with Cain Lawton. When questioned Isaac had to admit that "he was not sober" at the time.

Still on the evidence of the fight, Sarah Lloyd, wife of James Lloyd, a collier living in Church Street, said that on the night of 19th December a little before 12 o'clock, Lawton and Brindley had entered her house to light their pipes. Having stayed a few minutes, they left. She had escorted them to the door and had seen two other men in the street. She did not know either of them, but suddenly one of them struck Cain Lawton and knocked him down. While he was still on the ground, she heard his attacker say that he would "cut his ***** head off".

So far the jury could be certain that Ratcliffe and Luke had attacked Lawton, but the only evidence was of an attack in Church Street, and Lawton had walked away from that assault. Beyond that there were only the reported remarks of Ratcliffe and Luke about a scuffle and "black flesh". Had the two followed him and carried out a more ferocious attack?

Thomas Whittles was forge man. He told the court that on the night of 19th December he was acting as the watchman at the Silverdale Forges. Some time after midnight but long before daylight, he saw two men coming from the direction of the Rompin Pit. One of them was Ratcliffe. They had paused within five yards of him and he had wished them "good morning", speaking to Ratcliffe in particular.

At that point in Whittles' evidence Ratcliffe shouted out, "You never spoke to me in your life, at least not that morning!" Whittles ignored the interruption and continued with his evidence. He told the jury that the prisoner had replied, but he could not remember his exact words.

Asked by a juryman how he could be certain that one of the men was the prisoner, Whittles said that he could see him clearly as it was a moonlit night, and the glow from his furnace showed up the prisoner's face. Also with snow on the ground, it made things lighter. He had known the prisoner for about a year and he was sure that it was him.

From a comprehensive plan laid out on a courtroom table, Whittles clearly showed the jury that the two men had walked down the road that led directly from the Rompin Pit. He also told the jury that what kept the memory of Ratcliffe in his mind was the fact that the prisoner had never spoken to him before that fatal night. It was that fact and hearing about the body which jogged his memory.

The next witness, Samuel Forrester, was so nervous that he told the court his name was Forster. Ratcliffe immediately created a scene with much commotion and "merriment", according to the *Sentinel's* reporter, when he claimed that a witness who did not even know his own name could hardly give evidence against anyone else. The Coroner had difficulty calming the courtroom but eventually Forrester was allowed to continue.

On the Monday after Christmas Day, Forrester had said to Ratcliffe while in the pit, "You must have been one who helped to kill Cain Lawton?" Ratcliffe had become very angry and replied that if the witness ever spoke like that again, he would "blow up the pit". Because of that threat, Forrester told the court that he was afraid to go to work the following day. However, Ratcliffe had come to his house that evening and threatened that if he did not return to work, the manager would summon him.

Added to that evidence, Forrester said that he remembered being in Parton's beer house on Newmarket Day [the race meeting] when a man offered to bet Ratcliffe some money that Cain Lawton would never been found alive. Ratcliffe said that he would bet that Lawton had gone to Newchapel. Encouraged by his renewed confidence, Forrester stated that recently he had often seen Ratcliffe crying and cursing, saying that he hoped they would find Lawton and "get this job over". He had never seen Ratcliffe cry before Lawton's disappearance.

Was Ratcliffe's conscience altering his behaviour? Another witness would testify to his being erratic.

Mary Parton was wife of the landlord of the Castle Tavern at Newcastle. She said that Ratcliffe and other men were in the tavern on Newmarket Night when there was a great row. One of the men accused Ratcliffe of being a murderer, saying that Ratcliffe knew that Cain Lawton would never turn up again alive because he knew that Lawton was dead. The same man demanded to know from Ratcliffe where Lawton was, to which Ratcliffe replied that he had "gone on the road with some woman". But Ratcliffe would not say who the woman was or where they had gone.

Mary Parton added that Ratcliffe had told his accuser the same thing once before. Being accused at a private house, he had followed the man outside and knocked him down. While the man was down, a friend had kicked him. He had not said who had done the kicking and she could not recognise the other prisoner, Luke, as Ratcliffe's associate.

So far William Luke had been identified as attacking Lawton in Church Street, but at no other point. Then came the ambiguous but vaguely suggestive evidence of John William Kent, a shoemaker living at Brook Street, Silverdale where he lodged with the mother of William Luke. At her request he had written a letter to William Luke at Littleborough, and now produced a copy.

> "Silverdale, June 9th, 1875
>
> Dear son, this comes with all our kind respects to you and I must inform you that they have found Cain Lawton this morning (Wednesday) and they have found him in Rompin Engine Pit; and they say that he was quite naked, and his clothes with him and his boots he had with him. And they say that they are going to take Ratcliffe tonight so that you would not be surprised. They brought him up in a sheet. There is no one knows save your mother and me. If there is any disturbance we shall send you word.
>
> John Kent"

Under questioning Kent said that after Lawton vanished Luke had stayed in Silverdale for about four months. Before he went he had remarked that "it was strange that Lawton never turned up". So far as his own integrity was concerned, Kent told the court that as soon as he realised the seriousness of Luke's position he had shown the letter to the police. Also, he never had any "intention of giving Luke money to get away".

The letter seemed to suggest that Luke was implicated in Lawton's fate, but how? Did Mrs Luke know or suspect that her son and Radciffe had killed Lawton? The Coroner pointed out that Ratcliffe and another had been seen close to the shaft where Lawton's body was found and that they would find difficult to explain. However, no one could actually say that they had seen the two with Lawton near the pit. It was up to the jury to decide what they thought had happened.

The Coroner's jury soon agreed to indict Ratcliffe and Luke on charges of murder and were transferred to Stafford to await trial at the Assizes.

Despite their situation both men marched off through the crowds outside the Sneyd Arms and seemed totally unconcerned, exhibiting "considerable bravado". Some days later though, Ratcliffe was interviewed by a reporter from the *Staffordshire Sentinel* and his attitude had changed. He seemed "much affected" by his imminent trial at Stafford, while Luke still seemed unconcerned and told the reporter, "I think we shall have fair play there".

The trial began on 23rd July 1875 under Baron Pollock. It seems that no new witnesses appeared and the evidence given at the Coroner's hearing was repeated unchanged. There was clear evidence of an attack in Church Street, some evidence to show that Ratcliffe might have disposed of Lawton's body, but nothing that clearly indicated murder. And there was no explanation at all of why Lawton's clothes were removed, but not stolen – leaving money in his pockets, and thrown down the shaft after him.

Mr Underhill, for the Prosecution, told the jury that accidental death must be ruled out because the shaft was so well protected. Suicide was improbable because of the naked state of the corpse, the severed arm and the deceased's previous character. That left the only possibility – death was caused by other people and those people were the two prisoners. The only matter for the jury to decide was whether the prisoners killed Cain Lawton deliberately or whether he had died as a result of the drunken quarrel. The first would be wilful murder, the second manslaughter. He preferred the first.

Mr Young for the Defence agreed that the three men had fought, but told the jury that Lawton had simply walked away from that quarrel and had accidentally fallen down the shaft in his drunken and bruised state. There was no evidence that the prisoners had taken Lawton's body to the shaft and deposited it there. If they had done so, why had they passed many other shafts on the way? If his clients had killed Lawton near the shaft, why was there no evidence of a scuffle? Finally, why had no one seen blood on either of the prisoners if they had just killed the deceased?

There was no direct evidence to show that Ratcliffe and Luke had caused Lawton's death, either deliberately or by accident, only rather suspicious circumstances. Baron Pollock might have concluded that there was insufficient evidence to prove murder or manslaughter beyond reasonable doubt and directed the jury to acquit because the prosecution had not established their case. Instead he summed up and the jury retired. They deliberated for about a quarter of an hour then returned with a verdict of manslaughter against each of the prisoners.

Before passing sentence Baron Pollock remarked, "Whether it was your intention – I cannot suppose that it was – in the first instance to inflict so cruel an injury against a fellow creature is not now in question; but that both of you were engaged in the act has now been proved. I am unable to find any redeeming feature which ought to recommend a lighter sentence". Ratcliffe and Luke were sentenced to fifteen years penal servitude.

One of Her Drunken Tricks
(Walsall 1884 – Express & Star)

So many crimes involve a breakdown of relations between husband and wife, and perhaps the most pathetic cases arise through drink. Home life with any drunk is a living hell, but when it spills over into public view it becomes unbearable. And to many people it seems worse when a woman is the drunkard.

This may have been the reason why the judge was so lenient with Isaac Bailey after he had struck out and killed his wife on Friday 19th September 1884? Or perhaps he should have been acquitted.

When Isaac Bailey married his wife Mary Ann it was the second marriage for both of them. Isaac left his work as a "butty collier" and they had gone to keep a pub in Wolverhampton. It was there that their heavy drinking habits began, though Mary Ann Bailey far outstripped her husband. Realising what was happening to both of them, Isaac gave up his pub and they moved to Ryecroft in Walsall to open a small grocery shop and coal merchants.

They did well enough to be considered people of substantial property and highly respected members of the community. Isaac became primo of a lodge of the Royal Ancient Order of Buffaloes. Even so, drink gradually took over again, and though usually on good terms with one another, in one of their drinking bouts they frequently fell out, and often in public. Friends had to admit that it was Mary Ann who became violent and abusive, while her husband tried desperately to calm her down or ignore her drunken rages.

On the afternoon of 19th September 1884 Isaac was sitting in the bar of the Lord Raglan public house when his wife entered, visibly the worse for drink. There was a row in which she threatened to attacked Isaac, so the landlord, William Gough, took hold of her and pushed her out of the pub, causing her to stumble and fall and hit the back of her head on the pavement.

A friend of Mary Ann called Mary Slaney saw what happened, picked her up and escorted her back to the Baileys' shop. When they arrived Mrs Bailey refused to be quietened and was determined to go back to the Lord Raglan and "have it out" with the landlord, so she left Mary Slaney in charge of the shop with orders to lock up.

By the time she had closed the shop and found Mary Ann the argument between husband and wife had moved to the Union Inn in the same street as the shop. Mary Slaney did not want to be part of the quarrel and she was embarrassed by Mary Ann's foul language, so she quickly handed over the key and turned to leave. As she walked away she saw Isaac jump up. She did not see him hit his wife, but she did hear a thump on the floor, and when she turned around Mary Bailey was lying there.

Immediately she and the landlady went to help her friend up, but it was too late – Mary Ann Bailey was quite dead.

WIFE MURDER
AT
WALSALL
THIS AFTERNOON.

When Constable Cliffe arrived he questioned Isaac, who admitted hitting his wife. In fact he never denied this throughout his trial, but insisted that he only "gave her a push" or something similar. He explained that his wife was "troubled with heart disease" which may have caused her to die from the sudden fall, but the Constable arrested Isaac.

Throughout the inquest in the Coroner's Court, Isaac Bailey insisted that he struck his wife to stop her violence, but he had never intended to kill her. While the Coroner seemed to believe him, he had no option but to commit Isaac to Stafford Assizes for trial on a charge of murder.

When the trial opened Mr Justice Lucas said that the charge of murder should be dropped and replaced by one of manslaughter. It was never in doubt that Isaac Bailey had killed his wife, but also not in doubt was that he had never intended murder – there was no "malice aforethought". This rather quaint expression is still part of the textbook definition of murder and means an intention to kill or cause serious bodily harm. What had to be decided, the judge explained, was the true cause of death and who was really to blame.

The crucial witness as to the cause of death was a Dr Maclachlan, the surgeon who performed the post mortem at 10 o'clock on Saturday 20th September. He said that there had been no external injuries when he examined the body, but on removing the scalp he found three bruises with blood clots. The largest of those was on the back of the head, a little to the left side. There was a second bruise about two to three inches from the ear and a third was about the same as the second. He had also found a large effusion of blood starting in front and running to the back of the spinal cord.

Dr Maclachlan's opinion was Mrs Bailey's death was caused by the injury to the back of the head, probably due to a fall, which created the effusion of blood on the brain. He did admit that the blow might have caused the clot, but he favoured the fall as being the more likely cause of death.

Under cross examination he had to conclude that "the cause of death, the effusion of blood, must have taken place after the blow was administered", but he could not say definitely whether it was the blow or the fall which actually brought about the fatality.

This cast some doubt on whether the fall or Isaac's blow had actually killed Mary Ann Bailey. The judge wanted to find out how hard Isaac had hit his wife, but once again, the evidence was conflicting.

Phoebe Brittain, landlady of the Union Inn, was at first definite that Isaac used his fist, but she changed her story in court and admitted that she was not sure at all.

Charles Cocking was a sixteen year old lad who lived in the same street as the Union Inn. He was in the pub yard when Mrs Bailey climbed the steps towards her husband. He said that he clearly saw Isaac Bailey jump up and hit her with a clenched fist. The only other witness present in the bar was Mary Slaney who was adamant that she did not see the actual blow, only Mary Bailey lying on the steps.

It was then that the trial began to take a strange twist. Isaac's counsel, Mr Darling, began to argue that the whole incident was the fault of Mary Ann and that she had driven her husband to strike her. If she not been such a drunken, violent woman her death would never have taken place. The blame rested with her.

Mr Darling examined the events of the fatal afternoon and presented the jury with several witnesses to show what a dreadful woman Mary Ann had been. The judge never once questioned this line of approach.

William Gough was landlord of the Lord Raglan. Mrs Bailey, he said, had arrived there at about 4 o'clock that Friday afternoon and she was not sober. When her husband had refused to go home with her saying he would "come when I am ready" Mary Ann began to use foul language, and so Gough "put her out". However, she had come back in by another door and demanded a drink. Her husband had said, "Do not fill her any; she has had enough". Mary Ann then threatened to fight both Isaac and himself.

Gough swore that he heard Isaac Bailey say, "Keep away or I will strike you". That was deliberately said because she was trying to fight her husband. To calm the situation the landlord had again taken hold of Mary Ann and forced her into the street. That was when she had fallen down.

Another customer at the Lord Raglan at the time of the incident was Joseph Merrett, a baker. He agreed with all of Gough's account but added that when the landlord was putting Mary Ann out, she had caught hold of Gough's collar. As she was forced through the door she let go and toppled backwards, hitting her head on the ground. It was drink that had made her unsteady on her feet.

When the argument moved to the Union Inn, Phoebe Brittain swore that she had witnessed it all. Mrs Bailey had arrived at about ten minutes past four, "very much excited, her hair being disarranged, and she was considerably the worse for beer". There was no one else in the bar at the time except for the landlady. Mary Ann had gone to the back of the pub and down a flight of stone steps to the toilets. When she left the bar Isaac Bailey entered, but he had not ordered a drink. All he had done was search the bar and kitchen as if looking for someone.

As he reached the passageway that led to the steps he spotted his wife in the yard. Then he called for a pint. Mrs Brittain said that she had refused to serve him as she "did not wish any dispute in her house", and asked him to go home. By that time Mrs Bailey was at the top of the steps and had begun to swear at her husband. He retaliated by calling her a "drunken cat".

When Mary Ann carried on swearing at him, Isaac got up and struck her a blow on the left side of the head with his hand. Mrs Bailey fell onto the steps. Mrs Brittain shouted for her husband who was working in the cellar. He came up quickly and they both helped Mary Ann into a chair, not realising that she was already dead.

Sure that something dreadful had happened, she turned to Isaac Bailey and told him she thought his wife was dead. He said that his wife had been drinking down town all day and that her supposed death was "only one of her drunken tricks". Even so, Phoebe Brittain was afraid that it was not acting and persuaded her husband to fetch the police.

In his final speech Mr Darling said that his client had never disputed hitting Mary Ann, but had always denied wanting to kill her. The whole incident was an unfortunate accident in which Mrs Bailey was largely to blame. Mr Darling went so far as to argue that her death was caused not so much by the blow or the fall, but by her own violent temper. Had she not been so excited in her anger, she would still be alive. The vessels in her brain, Mr Darling theorised, were so weakened by continual drinking that they would have punctured at any time. Her fit of temper on that fatal afternoon had simply forced them to burst more quickly, resulting in her untimely death. It was an interesting idea, even if totally unsupported by any of the medical evidence.

It seems a strange approach in court, to blame the victim of someone charged with manslaughter for her own death. But she was a woman and a violent, drunken wife, and this was Victorian England where marriage meant female subservience. Mary Bailey had dared to humiliate her husband in public and almost deserved to pay the penalty.

The judge summed up the evidence and the jury delivered a very rapid verdict. Isaac Bailey was guilty of manslaughter, but they strongly recommended mercy on account of the provocation he had suffered.

The jury seem to have ignored the medical evidence which was quite inconclusive as to whether Isaac's blow had caused his wife's death, meaning that they could not be sure of his guilt beyond reasonable doubt. On the other hand the reference to provocation suggests that they gave some weight to Mr Darling's argument about Mary Ann's role in the drama.

Surprisingly, the judge said that he agreed. Before passing sentence he told the court that "he scarcely knew a case in which the circumstances were more extenuating". The defendant was guilty of the manslaughter of his wife, but deserved no more than "two days" in prison. Those, of course, he had already served awaiting trial and so he went free from the court.

The Curse of
Lame Joe Marshall
(West Bromwich 1871
Wolverhampton Chronicle)

The countryside has always whispered with tales of witchcraft, strange things in churchyards, malignant mists and frightful omens. Towns are supposed to be more sophisticated, but in the past they were no different. Miners were particularly fearful and superstitious, perhaps through working in the bowels of the earth, home of evil imps and goblins. Jon Raven tells many miners' stories in his book *Stories, Customs, Superstitions, Tales, Legends & Folklore of the Black Country & Staffordshire.*

Probably the worst that could happen to a miner was meeting some evil on his way to work. It could be prophesying his death if he continued. It was known for a miner to turn back and go home if he met a cross eyed woman on his way to the pit. Crossed eyes meant possession by the devil.

So what chance then did poor John Higginson have at his work? He was originally from the countryside but worked in the pits, and the one workmate he seemed to befriend was cross eyed.

Born in Tipton around 1830, John Higginson began his life as a farm labourer's lad. However, as he grew to manhood farm work did not pay enough and so he got a job at Hall End Pits, Church Lane, West Bromwich, owned by a Mr Alford. A well built, burly character, John could have gained the respect of his workmates, but he was shy and found it difficult to make friends. And he was rather slow or simple minded, which added to his discomfort with people. It was that which lead him into the clutches of Lame Joe Marshall.

Joe Marshall had worked most of his life at Hall End. In his youth he had been crippled by a mining accident and so Mr Alford, whose family felt responsible for him, had allowed him to stay on at the pit as a banksman. They also let him live in a small hut in the pit yard known locally as the hovel. With little money and no likelihood of ever earning much, Marshall had learned to live off his wits. It was that cunning which made John Higginson an obvious target.

Having studied his victim and learned all about him, Marshall made friends with Higginson and the pair of them often drank together in the Nag's Head Tavern. But there was something very odd about the friendship because

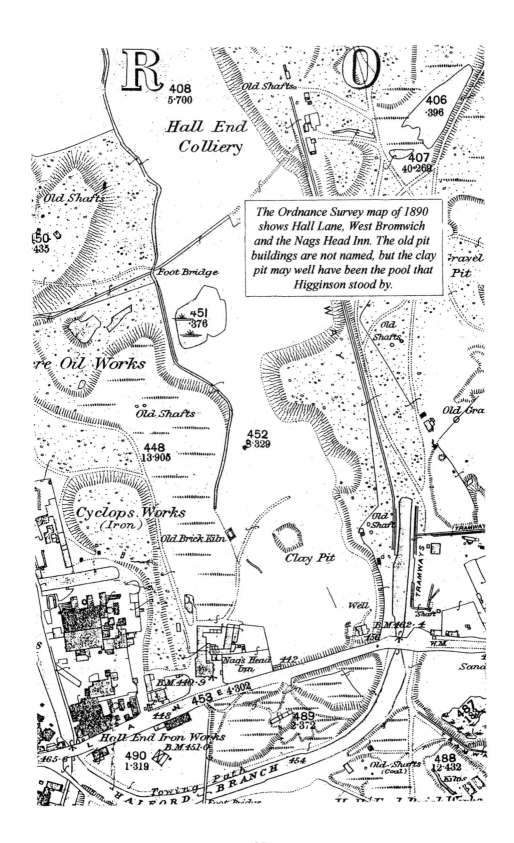

The Ordnance Survey map of 1890 shows Hall Lane, West Bromwich and the Nags Head Inn. The old pit buildings are not named, but the clay pit may well have been the pool that Higginson stood by.

Higginson always paid for the ale, never Marshall. It came out in the trial that Marshall had threatened to "put the evil eye on John" unless he kept him supplied with ale. So frightened was poor Higginson of the old cripple that he never complained to anyone. So what must have happened to make him suddenly wish his tormentor dead and commit the foul deed himself?

On the evening of 24th June 1871 the two were drinking in the Nag's Head. By the time they left both were drunk and deep in argument. Higginson went towards his lodgings at Mrs McEvoy's while Marshall returned to the hovel. A neighbour remembered seeing Marshall at about 11 o'clock and another swore that he heard him swearing some time about 5 in the morning. However, when Isaac Bloxidge called at the hovel on the morning of Sunday 25th June, he found Marshal lying on the ground in front of the fire.

Marshall's body had been partially burned and was still smouldering; only his head had escaped the fire. Thinking some dreadful accident had happened, Isaac ran for his friend James Timmis to help him examine the body. Having done that, they called the police.

When Constable Mollary arrived he found that Marshall had been beaten about the head with a blunt weapon. Blood was still oozing from the wounds, brain tissue was protruding from the head and his face was covered with blood. A search uncovered a hammer, two rakes, a spade and shovel. The hammer had blood on it and seemed to be the murder weapon.

The constable then went to Mrs McEvoy's house and asked Higginson to come to the police station. Here Higginson said that he had gone with Marshall to the canal side on the evening of 24th June but left him there. He admitted that he had left his lodgings in the night but had only gone over the pit mound to collect mushrooms, returning to the lodgings at about 3.30. But when Superintendent Woolaston examined Higginson's boots he found blood on them. The police were sure that they had their murderer.

The trial began at Stafford Assizes on 26th July under Mr Justice Lush. This came so soon after the crime because the police were convinced it was a straightforward and obvious case. However, one thing they had failed to establish was the motive for murder. What had made the prisoner kill his only friend and in such a gruesome manner?

The first witness was Elijah Gurney, a stoker at Hall End Pit who lived at the Wharfside, near the Nag's Head Tavern. On the night of 24th June he was in a house in Church Street at about 11.30 pm when he saw John Higginson and Joe Marshall together. They were walking in the direction of Hall End Tavern and arguing vehemently with one another. He swore that he heard Higginson threaten to "punch Marshall's head off", and Marshall's reply that he "would punch Higginson's off". By that time they had reached the canal. Marshall had gone towards the hovel and Higginson turned towards his lodgings. Both men were very drunk.

James Timmis lodged with the prisoner. He said that Higginson had arrived at the lodgings some time after 11.00 pm that Saturday evening and had gone to bed almost at once. Timmins had slept on the sofa. At about 3.00 am he was woken up by the prisoner who was just leaving the lodgings. When he asked Higginson where he was going the prisoner said, "I am going to get some mushrooms".

Higginson was away about three quarters of an hour and when he got back said that he had been unable to find any mushrooms and went back to bed. When questioned by counsel Timmis said that it was too dark for him to see how the prisoner looked. It was some time after that when Isaac Bloxidge came to the lodgings and asked him to come to Marshall's hovel, where he saw the burning corpse.

Sure that Higginson would want to know about his friend, Timmis went back to the lodgings and told him about "Joe's burning". Higginson seemed unmoved and Timmis asked him why he did not want to see his friend. The prisoner replied that he "did not care to see anyone who had been burnt, owing to a sight he had witnessed at an explosion". Despite several attempts Higginson would not be persuaded to visit the hovel.

Another witness named Moore said that he had promised Bloxidge that he would get the boiler at Hall End Pit going on that Saturday night, ready for the Sunday shift. He had arrived at the colliery at about 11.00 pm and started the boiler. Once lit, he had slept by its side until woken by the wind at about 2.00 am. Shortly after that he had seen the prisoner come out of the lodgings and go into the hovel, where Marshall lived. He had stayed there for about a quarter of an hour and then left for the lodgings.

About half an hour later Higginson came to the boiler room, but when Moore asked him why he was there he didn't answer. Instead, Higginson had gone down the pit bank towards a large pool. Moore watched him stay by the pool for ten minutes and then walk off over a meadow close by. Moore said it must have been about 5.30 am when he saw Higginson by the pool.

Another miner, William Cole, was the watchman at Red Grange Colliery. He had been on his rounds at about 3.00 am on that Sunday morning when he had seen the prisoner going in the direction of the hovel at Hall End Colliery.

So far it had been clearly established that Higginson had been at the hovel during that fatal night, but still no motive for murder had been suggested. When Mr Kite, the surgeon who examined the corpse, gave his evidence it might have thrown some light on the case, but it seemed too bizarre to have real importance.

Mr Kite found the body charred and burnt on the one side from ankle to armpit, as might have been expected if Marshall had been knocked out by a hammer blow to his head and fallen across the fire. However, what the surgeon found most unusual was the arrangement of coals around the body, which he thought had been placed deliberately to cause the precise burns found.

Despite Mr Kite's concerns, his strange suggestion was not followed up and the prosecution's case closed with little evidence of motive. When Mr Ashley spoke for the defence he exploited that point to the full. The prosecution had not produced one scrap of evidence that might suggest that his client had deliberately gone to the hovel that evening with intent to kill.

Summing up, Mr Justice Lush pointed out to the jury that there was little proof of motive or of intent to kill [making it murder], but if they believed that Higginson had killed Marshall in a fit of temper or during a heated and physical argument, then he was guilty of manslaughter. The jury agreed with the second proposition and returned a verdict of manslaughter. John Higginson was sentenced to penal servitude for life.

If Mr Kite's unusual evidence was lost on the court, it was certainly not lost on the local people who knew both men. Months after the trial, rumours began to spread about the real motive for the murder – witchcraft, or more correctly, the destruction of it.

During the trial Elijah Gurney had actually mentioned the possible cause of the argument as the two men walked towards the canal, but he was never questioned about its meaning. A terrified Higginson had said, "The t*** has sent Poll down for me", to which a worried Marshall had excitedly shouted, "It is a **** lie!"

What or who was "Poll"? Higginson was never in trouble with the police before and there was no mention of a woman named "Poll" in his life. So why was he so terrified? If "Poll" was their word for the Devil or evil spirits (short for poltergeist?), then did Higginson believe that Marshall had carried out his threat and cast the evil eye on him? If so, he needed to act immediately.

Customers of the Nag's Head knew how afraid Higginson was of Joe Marshall, and he had probably told them of the curse. Eventually one of them must have jokingly told Higginson of the "Sedgeley Wizard", an old man who knew much about white witchcraft and how its power could destroy evil. Poor, simple minded John in his desperation must have sought him out and, as rumour had it, told others of the wizard's advice.

Apparently the only way to rid yourself of possible black magic is to kill the one who has threatened it. To make absolutely sure that the evil power does not escape into another body, the dead corpse has to be destroyed by burning.

Could these rumours then supply the missing motive for murder, and the intent to kill? Had superstition and fear aggravated by Marshall's cunning and greed turned the once gentle giant, John Higginson, into a frenzied killer? If all this had emerged at the trial he might well have been convicted of murder and hanged. Or would the jury have accepted that a curse amounted to provocation and brought a verdict of manslaughter?

Above the Call of Duty?
(Willenhall 1864 – Wolverhampton Chronicle)

During early 1864 Willenhall town had been suffering a spate of drunken, rowdy behaviour, especially at weekends. Given its general reputation in the middle of the 19th century, this was a fairly normal state of affairs. Even so, the police had been instructed to keep a careful watch in case the bad behaviour broke out into anything more serious. Their brief was to move the offenders on and try to make them go home, but events in early May 1864 left the force angry and demoralised.

On the evening of 7th May 1864 at about 11.30 pm Thomas Lockley, aged 24, his brother George (21), and three friends, John Edwards (20), Joshua Stanley (24) and Joseph Willetts (19), were out on a typical weekend pub crawl and had gone into the Saracen's Head. Realising that the whole party were already quite drunk the landlord, Putnam, met them in the passageway and refused to serve them. George Lockley became abusive and pushed the landlord out of the way, determined to get a drink. To frighten them into leaving Putnam threatened to call the police, having seen Constable Lyons walk by only minutes before.

His threat seemed to work because the group left, but not before shouting that they were not scared of "any old constables or bobbies either".

From the Saracen's Head the party headed for the nearby Hope and Anchor where they arrived shortly before midnight. Again they were refused a drink and left minutes later. Lois Marston, daughter of the landlord, said that the group were noisy but they did not seem tipsy. She watched them leave and then saw them being spoken to by Constable Lyons, who was ordering them home. After a time, the group walked off in the direction of the Bull Ring.

Whether Constable Lyons was being over officious or simply following his instructions, he decided to head for the Bull Ring to make certain that the men were going home. When he got there he met William Lowe and stood talking to him close to a wall. Soon afterwards three of the rowdy group arrived in the Bull Ring and George Lockley began to abuse Lyons.

Lyons tried to arrest George Lockley and a fight developed in which the policeman was punched and kicked and took a blow on the side of the head from a brick. Lyons was rescued by Lowe and other passers by. Constables Dutton, Hooper and Hampton arrived and with Lyons, who refused any medical attention until the arrests were made, went to the Lockleys' house to arrest the men.

It was only after they had been arrested that Constable Lyons went for medical help. At about 1.00 am he arrived at Mr Hartill's surgery and was seen by Mr Thomas Wolverton, Hartill's young assistant. Wolverton cleaned and dressed the wound to Lyons's head and told him to report back on Monday 9th for medicine. On the Monday Hartill was still unavailable and he did not see Lyons until the Tuesday 10th May.

Willenhall's fine ornamental clock in the Market Place. There is nothing left of the Saracen's Head or the Nag's Head.

At this point he discovered a fracture, but it had caused too much damage and despite an operation, Lyons died a week later on May 18th. What had begun as a simple attack on a policeman turned into a case of murder against the gang of five men.

The trial of Thomas and George Lockley, Edwards, Stanley and Willetts for the murder of Constable Lyons began at Stafford Assizes in July 1864 under Mr Justice Shee. It was soon clear that it would hinge on whether the actions of Lyons were within his powers and therefore legal.

If the young policeman had acted beyond his powers of arrest in trying to detain the men only for swearing and loud behaviour, then it might be argued that he had actually caused the quarrel which developed into the attack on him. If they were simply resisting an unlawful arrest then the men might only be guilty of manslaughter.

Mr Boughey for the prosecution argued that any assault on a policeman showed that there was malice aforethought, that is, an intention to kill or cause serious harm, because the assailants must know that their victim was a policeman because of his uniform. That uniform would denote that he was on duty and therefore had the right to ask the men go home. Any attack that took place after this request was bound to be illegal, and if it so happened that the attack ended in the death of the officer, as that one did, then the assailants must be tried for murder and not manslaughter.

If accurately reported in the *Wolverhampton Chronicle*, this seemed a poor start. People might obviously attack policemen without intending to kill them or cause serious harm, and the uniform proves little.

Mr Boughey then called William Lowe to the witness box. Relying heavily on his evidence, the prosecution hoped to prove which of the five men were involved in the attack and, if possible, which of them hit Constable Lyons with the brick.

William Lowe was a key maker living at Little Island, Willenhall. It was about 12.15 pm on the Sunday morning when he was approached near the Bull Ring by Constable Lyons who stood talking to him. From the constable's actions and manner it became obvious that he wanted Lowe to stay with him, and he did so. As they talked, Thomas and George Lockley with Edwards came up the road. Without any provocation from Lyons George Lockley began to swear at the policeman and when asked to go home, he refused.

At that point Edwards tried to calm the situation by taking hold of George Lockley and persuading him to go, but Lockley still refused to move and the two began to struggle. It was then that Constable Lyons tried to arrest and handcuff Lockley. As they struggled they both fell to the ground.

When the policeman was on the ground, Edwards and both of the Lockleys started to kick, thump and hit him. It was George Lockley who struck the first blow, kicking the officer in the side of his body. Lowe managed to wrestle George from the constable, who was being held down by the others, but George broke free and raced back to continue the attack. By that time Lyons was on his feet and he hit George across the forehead with his staff. At that point George took out a knife, but Lowe managed to grab him.

It was then that Thomas Lockley threw something at the officer who fell to the ground shouting, "Lowe, they have nearly killed me!". But that did not stop the men and they continued the attack.

At that moment a passer-by called Thomas Pitt came to help Lowe and together they managed to get Lyons into a house close by, owned by a Mr Walton. However, despite his wounds Lyons would not let the matter drop, and he went outside again to confront Stanley who refused to go home. It was then that Lowe and Pitt persuaded Lyons to go into the police station. As they were about to leave the scene another officer, Constable Dutton, arrived.

With backup, Lyons was determined to arrest the men and he and Dutton, with Lowe who knew where the Lockleys lived, headed towards Monmore Lane and the Lockleys' house. On the way, they met Stanley and arrested him. Further on they were joined by officers Hooper and Hampton. When they were refused entry they broke down the door to arrest both the Lockley brothers and Edwards.

Lowe's evidence was compelling and removed any doubt that four of the men had indeed attacked Lyons, while Willetts seems to have been just a bystander. However, what Lowe was uncertain about was what, if anything, Thomas Lockley had thrown at Lyons. He had seen Lockley's arm raised and presumed that he had thrown an object because the motion was like that of throwing, but he had not actually seen anything leave the hand. (Later one Eli Vaughan found a blood covered brick near the spot where the constable fell.)

William Lowe was never really cross examined by counsel for the defence and neither were other prosecution witnesses because the facts of the fight and its details were not in dispute. But what was questioned was whether the attack on the young police officer actually caused his death, or whether it was the result of the poor medical attention.

More interested in arresting his attackers, Constable Lyons had not looked for medical attention until they were locked in their cells. It was over an hour later when he arrived at the surgery of Mr Hartill. Unfortunately the experienced surgeon was not there and Lyons was seen by his junior, Mr Wolverton.

Wolverton gave evidence that he had cut the blood matted hair from around the wound, but as there was no fire in the surgery they had gone to the police station to dress the wound. In his opinion the wound was superficial because all that he found was a laceration in the scalp about one and a half inches long on the left side of the head. There were scratches on the cheek and the policeman's knuckles were bleeding.

When Constable Lyons complained again later about the head wound, Mr Wolverton again treated him because Hartill was still not available. He gave some medicine for the headache but still thought that the injury not worth bothering his senior partner with because he never suspected a fracture.

However, by Tuesday 10th Lyons called on Mr Hartill to examine him again. By that time, Lyons was suffering from loss of power and numbness in his right arm, but even the experienced doctor thought that there was nothing seriously wrong and all would be well. By Wednesday 11th Lyons had lost his speech so Mr Hartill examined the wound minutely and only then discovered a fracture.

Hartill operated immediately, removing nine pieces of splintered bone from the wound including one almost the size of a shilling piece. [10p piece] The operation seemed successful and Hartill had every confidence that Lyons, being a strong, young man, would recover. Even so, Lyons took a turn for the worse and died on Wednesday 18th.

Under cross examination Hartill refused to blame his young assistant. He insisted that the constable's wound in itself was not usually fatal and blamed Lyons for his refusal to seek medical help immediately and his continued fighting after the blow, which had made the situation far worse. Hartill insisted that they had done all in their power to save the young officer.

Mr Johnstone Neale for the defence was not satisfied. He argued that it was the criminal lack of good medical care that had cost Lyons his life, particularly where Mr Wolverton was concerned. In a highly emotional speech he accused Mr Wolverton of "disgusting charlatanism" in his failure to consult the more knowledgeable partner and even suggested that if anyone should be in the dock for manslaughter it should be the two doctors.

As to his own clients, Mr Neale admitted that there was no argument that they were involved in the fight, but if Constable Lyons had not provoked them, then the sad incident would never have happened. He suggested that rather than being commended for his actions, Constable Lyons acted very rashly and should be condemned for attempting to arrest the men.

Growing more impassioned, he quoted the early 18th century judge Lord Holt, on an English citizen's rights, "When an illegal arrest took place it was a challenge to all England. It defied our birthright – Freedom". [And see below for another memorable quotation.] Johnson Neale continued that if Lyons' arrest were legal, then it would mean "the people of England were to become slaves of their servants and their liberties were gone forever".

Clearly, it was a difficult case and Mr Justice Shee took great pains when he summed up the law and the evidence. However, if the *Wolverhampton Chronicle's* report is strictly accurate he trespassed a long way into the jury's territory of deciding the facts.

First he dismissed death through lack of medical care, saying that the wound was a mortal one and Constable Lyons would have died anyway. Secondly, in his opinion the arrest by Lyons was an illegal act "George Lockley was not doing anything that in point of law would justify apprehension, and therefore he had a right to resist. But more importantly, if the prisoners, with common intent, persisted in their violence after the policeman was disabled, and they knew he was disabled, and tried to stop his arresting one of their number, even though it was an illegal arrest, then they would be guilty because the officer would no longer be acting illegally, but doing his duty."

If the officer died as a result of the attack then they could be guilty of murder, but malice aforethought had to be proved. The judge felt certain that the death was caused by the fight but was more inclined to favour manslaughter and saw no reason why the prisoners should be excused. They were, he said, guilty in varying degrees with Willetts seemingly little more than an onlooker and Thomas Lockley responsible for the actual wound.

After half an hour, not long in such a complicated and important case, the jury found the two Lockleys, Edwards and Stanley, guilty of manslaughter. Stanley was recommended for mercy because of his otherwise good character and Willetts they found not guilty. Thomas Lockley was goaled for eight years, his brother and Edwards for six, and Stanley for five years.

The Willenhall Police were angry. They were convinced that Constable Lyons had been murdered and that the Willenhall louts had gained yet another victory. They felt that without backing from the courts further violence would flourish, and especially against the police.

Many people will sympathise with this view, but the courts are there to decide, impartially, whether people are guilty of the crime charged, rather than support the police or any wider objective. It is hard to disagree with the verdict of manslaughter and the sentences were not light.

Even so, the Willenhall Police were right in thinking that there would be more trouble on the streets. A year later Constable Hooper, who had gone to help Lyons, was himself killed in a brawl with a drunken gang, and his killer was acquitted. Hooper's case appears in *Midland Murders & Mysteries* by Barrie Roberts , also published by QuercuS.

[**Lord Holt** once became infuriated with the inaccurate and misleading reports of past cases which were common at the time. "These scrambling reports," he burst out, " posterity will take us for a parcel of blockheads."]

Victoria Intervenes
(Wolverhampton 1886 – Express & Star)

Reprieves from the death sentence were rare in Victorian times, but the public outcry which followed the conviction of William Narrowmore in 1886 provided one example. Perhaps it was not a very desirable one.

Narrowmore was a 27 year old nail maker. He had married 20 year old Harriet Carter some three years earlier but it was not a happy union. In the short time they were married they separated seven times, William returning to his parents and Harriet to hers. Each blamed the failure of their marriage on infidelity by the other, though no evidence was ever found against William.

By late September 1886 they had separated again and Harriet was back at her mother's home. On Friday 8th October William had gone to Mrs Carter's house and there was an argument between himself and his wife. He had left, but returned again on the Sunday evening after his regular prayer meeting with the Salvation Army.

That evening they had an explosive row in the street which was seen by several neighbours. They had a fight and Harriet scratched William's face, making it bleed. Whether he struck Harriet or not was never proved, but he left in a very angry mood.

The following evening, Monday 11th, Willam once again visited the Carter house and demanded to see his wife. Despite warnings from her mother, Harriet decided to go for a walk with William. At around 10 o'clock the pair set off down Oxford Street seeming perfectly amicable. Even so, Harriet's sister was not happy and she persuaded several neighbours to come with her while she followed the couple. At a spot near Lover's Lane they decided that nothing was wrong and turned back.

At 7.40 on the Tuesday morning a boatman, Edward Jones from Walsall Street, found Harriet's body floating in the Birmingham Canal between Horsley Fields Bridge and the Iron Bridge. Her corpse was moved to the mortuary in Corporation Street and later identified by William.

Although at the mortuary he seemed shocked, investigations led the police to detain William later that day on suspicion of causing his wife's death. While at the police station William made a very lengthy statement, some of which was as follows:

"I met Harriet Narrowmore, my wife, in Oxford Street at about nine-thirty p.m. on Monday 11th, and walked with her to the end of Union Street, Horsley Fields. She said, "I am glad I have seen you because I have been to Mrs Chambers who was formerly head of the St George's Church Army, and I have repented tonight and I intend to lead a better life in future." She said, "I don't want to go far tonight because I am afraid we shall meet that young man that I have been going with and he said that he would knock your brains out if he saw you with me again." She said, "Bill, I have never done you any good, but if you will live with me again after this time, I will try and make you a good wife in the future."

The statement continued:

"She said, "I am afraid I am in trouble and before I would go with him again and get myself disgraced, I would sooner beg bread and walk on the road. If I was to die tonight, I would have to tell my mother as she has been the cause of me going off with that other man. If something is not done, you will find me missing."

I said, "Dear wife, never think of doing anything to yourself because you are away from me and they will think that it is me that has done it."

She said, "If you will come tomorrow night at half past seven, I will be in the house."

So I left her in Union Street about ten o'clock. I heard no more of her till nearly eight o'clock on Tuesday morning when her sister, Eliza, came to my house and said, "Harriet has not come home all night".

Another sister, Maria, also came later. I said, "Tell your mother I will willingly go to the police station if they want me".

This seems a very full and detailed statement from someone just detained for his wife's murder, and rather favourably worded. The police were suspicious, but could they actually find evidence that might convict William Narrowmore? To all intents and purposes he was the victim – a respected member of the Salvation Army whose wife had been unfaithful. Had this devout Christian been driven to commit murder?

From the outset it seemed that Narrowmore portrayed himself as the wronged partner. At the Magistrates' Court on Wednesday 13th he first appeared "somewhat indifferent", throwing his hat carelessly on the seat, but when the charge was read out "he burst into an immoderate fit of crying and stamped his feet in a paroxysm of grief".

99

See map page 102.

*Looking through the
"Iron Bridge" to
Horseley Fields Bridge.*

He was not so grief stricken that he had lost his reason. Narrowmore was wise enough to make clear to the court that the scratches on his face were there before the Monday evening. Police Constable Kendrick who had taken him to the mortuary confirmed that fact. And he asked the court for a favour before his next appearance. Loudly enough for everyone to hear he asked that he might be allowed "before I go to Stafford, to see Mrs Chambers", a lady well known in Wolverhampton as a devout Salvation Army leader. If that were not enough, as he left the dock for the cells Narrowmore was heard to say to his sister, "Never mind, I am happy I shall go to Heaven".

Whether Narrowmore was deliberately playing to the gallery could never be proved, but the case attracted such local interest that for his next appearance the court was "crowded to excess and large numbers were unable to gain admission". Once again, they saw a man humbled by an unfaithful wife and driven to despair. Their reaction later proved beneficial to Narrowmore..

On Thursday 14th October the Coroner, Mr Phillips, opened the inquest at the Town Hall. Enough witnesses seemed to have been found for him to establish how Harriet Narrowmore had died, but the case began badly. The police surgeon, Mr Winter, had only made an external examination of the body as it lay in the coffin and had not discovered any traces of violence. Annoyed, the coroner ordered him to make an immediate post mortem.

Unwilling to adjourn the hearing at this stage, Mr Phillips called the next witness. Eliza Clarke of 20 Oxford Street, was Harriet's sister. She told the court that William and her sister had been married for three years but had lived together for only some of that time. The couple had separated frequently and for the last year Harriet had lived alternately at the homes of her parents and William's parents.

On Monday 13th October Eliza and Harriet returned home from work at Messrs Bayliss in Monmore Green at 5.30 pm. Harriet then went out to a meeting of the Church Army of which she had been a member for fifteen months. Returning home at about 9.30 she brought with her a fish supper. Shortly before 10 o'clock William arrived asking to speak to Harriet. She had borrowed a shawl from her mother and gone out with him down Oxford Street.

Fearful for her sister's safety because William was acting strangely, Eliza decided to follow the couple with some neighbours. By the time they had reached Lover's Lane in Cornhill she decided that all was well and turned back for home. When Harriet did not come home that evening she went to William's mother's house. There William told her, "I was in bed before 10 o'clock. I left her at the top of Oxford Street."

Questioned by the jury, Eliza was certain that the couple had left her home just "as the clock was striking ten". As to the scratches on William's face, she admitted that they were caused on the Sunday evening. William had struck Harriet and she had retaliated. Their argument had been about Harriet seeing another man, Thomas Atkinson.

Was William or Eliza telling the truth about the time? The next witness was Isaac James Jenks, a striker of Alma Street. On the Monday evening at about 20 minutes to 11 he had seen a couple walking along the canal towpath near the railway bridge. He noticed that the woman wore a shawl and that she was taller than the man. The man had a moustache. Isaac swore that he knew the man from the Salvation Army and that it was the prisoner.

Another witness, Jane Chilton of Oxford Street, said that on the Monday night at about half past 11 she had gone to her front door and seen Narrowmore standing near Mrs Carter's window. He seemed to be trying to look through the shutters, which were closed. This was never mentioned again and never explained.

Walter Haltham was a boot finisher of 35 Oxford Street. On the Monday evening at about 10 o'clock he was standing talking to William Dodd outside 23 Oxford Street. Eliza Clarke came up and asked them to come with her to follow William Narrowmore and his wife, because she thought her sister was in danger. They agreed and the three followed the couple as far as Lover's Lane. When William and Harriet seemed to be "walking gently side by side" they decided to stop following them. They last saw the couple just before they reached the iron bridge by the canal.

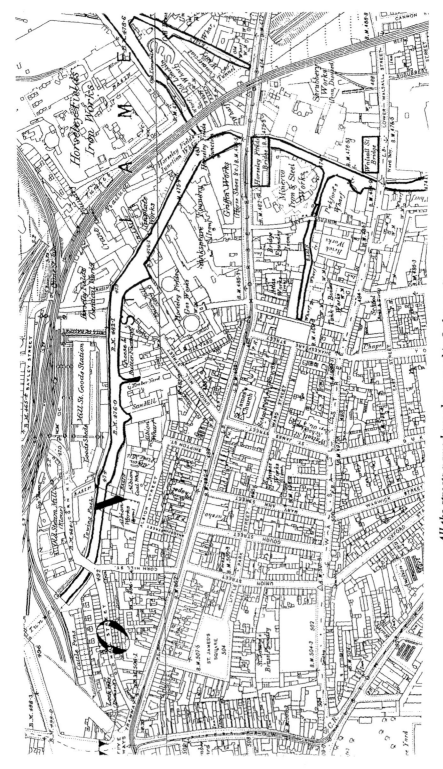

All the streets named are shown on this Ordnance Survey Map of 1898. For clarity the canal has been emphasised and the bridges were Harriet Narrowmore was found are boxed.

The next witness was Emma Narrowmore, William's mother, whose evidence disagreed with what the inquest had heard so far. She told the court that her son had been at home at 41 Park Street shortly after 10 o'clock. She described how she had met Harriet that same evening in the fish shop, and they had argued. Leaving the shop they met William and at his mother's request, he went home with her to Park Street. However, as she poured him a cup of tea he left, saying that he must speak with Harriet and that he would be only a few minutes. He returned between 10 and a quarter past.

To support her story Emma Narrowmore said that her other son, George, was in the house when William returned. George had reprimanded his brother for "following his wife about". When questioned, Emma had to admit that she had been in bed when William returned. Had she fallen to sleep and not known the exact time? George was equally unhelpful as to the exact time when William returned.

The court then heard of the many disputes between William and Harriet and how the neighbours had grown used to the quarrels and the inevitable reconciliations. Perhaps that was why the three followers turned back from Lover's Lane on the Monday evening, having decided the row was over. But that weekend's rows, and no one could have guessed, were probably the final straws that broke William's resistance.

Jane Poole lodged with Mrs Carter. On the Sunday evening Harriet had come home and said that Bill (Jane's husband), his brother and sister had "set about her". Harriet said that she was determined to find out why and had gone out into the street to confront them. There though, she met William and they had a fight with Harriet scratching William's face, but the witness never mentioned Harriet being struck.

More alarming though, Jane Poole told the court that on the previous Friday evening William had come into the Carter house and confronted Harriet. He told her that "she must either go and live with him comfortably or he would shorten her days". The pair left the house still rowing.

Thomas Atkinson was a striker from Westbury Street and Harriet's supposed lover. He had seen Harriet on the Sunday afternoon and they had walked together in Springfields until about half past 3. He had seen her again at 20 minutes to 10 at the bottom of Piper's Row and they had gone into the Barrel for a drink. While there, someone came in and Harriet left. He overheard a quarrel between the two and he was sure that the man's voice belonged to William Narrowmore, though he never saw him. Not wanting to be seen, he left by another door.

The Sunday fight also involved the police. Constable John Sergeant was on duty in Park Street when William called him into his house. He was bleeding from the cheek and told the constable that his wife had assaulted him. When Sergeant spoke to Harriet she complained that William was pestering her. With her husband present, she told the constable that she no longer wanted him.

Their argument continued in front of the constable, with William accusing his wife of infidelity. She retorted that he was also unfaithful. However, despite the heated argument William never became violent and Constable Sergeant left them, still arguing.

More startling evidence was to come about William's attitude to his wife. William Arnold, an edge tool polisher from Oxford Street, said that he knew both William and his wife from the Church Army meetings. Three Sundays before the tragedy William Narrowmore had told him that Harriet had ruined his life by her behaviour. He said that "she has done wrong many times" and that had led to their home being broken up three times and them separating on five occasions. Narrowmore then said that he "would take his wife's life", but Arnold warned him never to speak about it again or he would tell the police.

On 11th October Harriet told William Arnold that "she didn't know what to do as she was very weary of herself". She had begun to cry as she told him that she had once more separated from William, though by the time she left the church she had calmed down and "seemed not over-excited".

Another witness was Charles Burt, a moulder from 43 Park Street. On the nigh of Sunday 10th October he met William Narrowmore at the top of Oxford Street, and Narrowmore had said to him, "I tried to get Harriet down by the cut Friday night to see if I could drown her", adding "it will come to a bad end before it is settled".

Later the same evening Burt saw the commotion in Oxford Street when Harriet scratched her husband. Narrowmore had not hit back but walked away with Burt. During that walk Narrowmore had said, "If I had got my hands round her neck I had two minds to throttle her".

On the Monday Burt was in Bilston Street when he again met Narrowmore. He told Burt that he had been to try to get a separation from his wife. While they talked Josiah Dale came up and inquired about Narrowmore's wife, to which the prisoner replied that he would "drown her or knife her, one of the two, before all was over".

When questioned about Harriet's behaviour, Charles Burt said that he had never heard her talk of harming herself. She had always seemed as though she were in no trouble at all.

The court had now heard from all the available witnesses but they were still without medical evidence as to the cause of death. Rather oddly, the Coroner decided to conclude the inquest. He summed up the facts carefully, advising the jury that they were there only to say how the deceased met her death, and not to find anyone guilty or innocent. They could, however, recommend future action.

Within 10 minutes the jury returned a finding that Harriet Narrowmore had died from drowning, but that there was not sufficient evidence to show how she came by her death. Even so, they recommended that William Narrowmore be placed in custody to await trial at Stafford Assizes.

The trial began on 4th November under Mr Justice Matthew, and once again William Narrowmore seemed to be trying to play on the emotions of people in court. As he entered the dock he appeared perfectly self-possessed, but as soon as the jury members were sworn in he "wept copiously, drying his eyes with his handkerchief".

Could it work? It might have done but for Mrs Chambers, the Salvation Army leader whom Narrowmore had asked to see when he was remanded in custody by the magistrates. She had not appeared at the Coroner's Court because she claimed that anything said to her in confidence because of her religious position, like the Catholic confessional, could not be repeated. At Stafford Assizes she had pleaded with the court not to force her to "sin against her own conscience" but Mr Justice Mathew ruled that her evidence was "not privileged". "If the Crown insist on requiring your evidence, you are bound to give it".

What she had to say was devastating. Mrs Chambers told the court that on 13th October she had an interview with Narrowmore while he was in the cells. When she asked him if Harriet had gone "into the presence of god herself", the prisoner replied that he had "done it". She believed him because at the time, both of them were on their knees praying for God's forgiveness.

If that evidence were not sufficient, the police had another witness. John Aston, a labourer, had been placed in the same cell at Wolverhampton as Narrowmore. He told the court that he had asked the prisoner if he was "the man that's drowned his wife", to which Narrowmore had replied, "Yes. I was walking along the canal side and I was with her against some works. I was frightened someone was coming and we went walking on, she being nearest to the canal side. I pushed my foot out and she went over into the canal. I should have stopped to get her out, but I thought there was somebody behind close enough to save her. If you won't split, I will treat you if I get out. I don't care if they only give me five years."

The only other new evidence came from the surgeon, Mr Winter. His post mortem had revealed no evidence of external violence. The woman's arms were "rigid and fixed" as if she had been struggling, but that could have resulted from refusing to have sex rather than the drowning.

> ### THE WOLVERHAMPTON
> # WIFE MURDER.
>
> ## TRIAL OF THE PRISONER.
>
> ### SENSATIONAL EVIDENCE.
>
> ### CONFESSION BY THE PRISONER.
>
> ## SENTENCE OF DEATH.

Despite an impassioned plea from Mr Plumtre, counsel for the Defence, the jury were convinced that Narrowmore was guilty of murder but added a strong recommendation for mercy. The judge rejected this, saying that Narrowmore "had a desire to take the poor woman's life" and "without a moment's warning had hurled her out of this world into the presence of her maker". Consequently he "must be prepared to follow her". He passed the death sentence on William Narrowmore, to be carried out on 24th November 1886.

That should have been the end for William Narrowmore, but the people of Wolverhampton had taken the "poor man" to their hearts, and felt that he was as much victim as culprit. Within days a petition had been organised asking for a reprieve of William's death sentence, and within the week it had over ten thousand signatures. It was important that they included the names of most of Wolverhampton's influential citizens.

On 15th November the petition was sent to the Home Secretary together with testimonials from the Church Army, Mrs Chambers, Narrowmore's employers, Mr Winter, the surgeon, and many others who spoke of his good character.

With these documents was the following letter:

"I beg most respectfully to inform you that the very large and influentially signed petitions are but a slight indication of the very general feeling of sympathy with the prisoner in this district, and if Her Majesty can see her way to reduce the punishment to a short term of imprisonment, it is the universal opinion hereabouts that justice will be amply satisfied."

Mr R Rhodes
Solicitor

By 20th November the Home Office had replied:

"Sir, In reply to your telegram respecting the convict, William Narrowmore, who was sentenced to death for murder. I am instructed by the Secretary of State to acquaint you that he had advised Her Majesty to respite the capital sentence with the view to its commutation to penal servitude for life. I am, sir, your obedient servant,

Godfrey Lushington

Queen Victoria duly signed. The people of Wolverhampton might not have been completely satisfied, but a rather fortunate William Narrowmore escaped the fate that his wife had suffered.

THE
WOLVERHAMPTON
MURDER.

RESPITE
OF
NARROWMORE.

LETTER FROM THE PRISONER.

Beer and Ice Cream
(Wolverhampton 1888 – Express & Star)

Racial prejudice is not a late twentieth century phenomenon, as Italians living in Wolverhampton in the 1880s could have told you. Even so, no one had expected it would lead to murder.

On the evening of Monday 30th July 1888 a group of local youths left the Invincible Inn in Duke Street at 11 o'clock and began to walk down Cleveland Road towards Monmore Green, where most of them lived. As they were opposite the carriage factory of Forder and Co, they spotted a group of Italian ice cream sellers on their way home from Bilston rouse.

What happened next was not entirely clear, but an argument broke out and several blows were struck. The Italians managed to break free and started to run away. When the two groups were a fair distance apart the abuse continued until the Italians started to throw glasses at the local lads. At that point they decided to chase the Italians, perhaps to teach them a lesson. However, as the last Italian reached Mr Cund's carriage works he turned and confronted the leading chaser, Alfred Bateman.

Unable to stop, Bateman ran into the Italian but suddenly fell backwards shouting, "I've got it!" The Italian turned and ran followed by some of the youths. Meanwhile, Constable Newns heard the disturbance and began to make his way towards the noise. As he neared the street he heard cries of "Stop him!" and saw a man running towards him. He stopped the man and was soon surrounded by a group of people who accused him of stabbing their friend.

As he was taking the Italian back to Cleveland Road they came upon Bateman lying on the pavement. He examined him and found a knife wound, then he instructed the others to take the injured man to hospital. Bateman was still alive at that point but died on arrival at the hospital.

With Bateman and his friends on their way to hospital, Constable Newns took his prisoner to the police station. There he was told that Bateman had died and he promptly charged the Italian with murder. In his initial statement Antonio Ferrito denied that he was the man who had killed the Englishman, stating that he was merely running away when he had bumped into the policeman. Despite his protests, he was placed in the cells to await a Magistrates' Court hearing.

News soon spread of the attack and the town began to seethe with hatred for the foreigners. No one believed that the local youths had caused the affray and for a while the Italians were terrified of reprisals. The local press, for reasons only known to themselves, fuelled the town's anger with biased reporting, such as "it is not in the nature of Englishmen to tolerate the assaults of foreigners" and "the short temper, so characteristic of the Italian race, soon made itself manifest". This was obviously likely to persuade the people of Wolverhampton to believe that young Bateman was the innocent victim of a vicious crime. What chance did Ferrito have of a fair trial?

HORRIBLE MURDER

IN

WOLVERHAMPTON.

AN ENGLISHMAN

FATALLY STABBED

BY AN ITALIAN.

Ferrito had been remanded in custody on 1st August and the Borough Coroner, Mr W H Philips opened the inquest on 4th August. He knew that it would be difficult to find out exactly what had happened on the fatal evening because few witnesses had come forward who could be considered impartial. Prejudice seemed bound to colour the evidence of the opposing groups. However, Mr Philips was determined to maintain the neutrality of the law.

The first person to give evidence was Ruth Bateman, mother of the dead youth. She said that her 19 year old son had left their home at 23 Eagle Street just before 8 o'clock on the Monday evening. He had promised her that he would not be out late as he did not have much money. At 11.30 she was told of his death and went to the hospital to identify the body. Throughout her statement she insisted that Alfred was a good, hard working lad who had never been in any trouble.

The next witness was Charles Pickford, an ironplate worker living at 74 Dartmouth Street who was first of the many youths to give evidence. He had been in the pub with Bateman from around 9 o'clock until 11. At closing time the whole group left and started to walk up Bilston Street towards Steelhouse Lane. On their way they met a party of Italians, each one pushing an ice cream cart.

It was his brother, John Pickford, who said, "We'll have a pennyworth of ice cream" and placed the money on one of the carts. The cart's owner was tall and dark with black curly hair and Charles thought his name was "Steve something", though he could not be certain. The Italian refused to serve his brother and also, Pickford said, to return the money. An argument broke out, during which the Italian struck at Bateman but missed. Bateman retaliated, but also missed.

After that the Italians ran off up Cleveland Road, but they stopped about 20 to 30 yards away and started to throw ice cream glasses at the youths. One glass hit Sam White's wrist and damaged it, and so a chase began. Bateman caught up with the last Italian who let go of his cart and turned on Bateman. Suddenly Alfred fell backwards shouting that he had been stabbed. Having seen the lad fall, the Italian ran off, but Charles Pickford chased him until the policeman stopped the Italian. At no time did Charles lose sight of the man he was chasing.

Under cross-examination, Charles swore that he had enough light from a street lamp to see the attacker clearly. The Italian was wearing a white slop (a short smock, the type worn by cooks) and corduroy trousers. He was the only one wearing a slop, the others being in shirt sleeves.

Despite prolonged questioning, Charles maintained that the accused was the attacker and not one of the other Italians. He insisted that it was the Italians who started the argument and first used violence. He denied that anyone in his group had taken off a belt to hit the Italian, or that he might have been confused because of the drink he had supped that night. He was adamant that everyone in his party was sober.

Sam White, whose wrist was damaged, was a riveter at Fletcher's works. His evidence confirmed all that Charles Pickford had said, but it introduced the first elements of uncertainty in the case. White told much the same story of the incident and agreed that Bateman's attacker wore a slop, but could not be sure he was the only one in such a garment. Interestingly, he described the attacker as having a moustache and being short, but was not sure if he had curly hair or black eyes.

The only other witness called that day was Constable Newns. He told how he came to arrest Ferrito as the Italian ran along Snowhill. Unfortunately, after he had stopped Ferrito he had marched him back to the crime scene in Cleveland Road in full view of all his accusers. So it might be that the youths, wanting revenge on an Italian, decided that Ferrito would do?

Constable Newns said that Ferrito pleaded that the wrong man had been arrested and another Italian was the attacker, and certainly the police found no signs of blood on Ferrito's clothing or his hands. Surely some would appear after such a close encounter with the victim? Also, the weapon was never found, despite a lengthy search. If Charles Pickford never let Ferrito out of his sight, how did he dispose of the weapon?

The case was beginning to revolve around whether they had arrested the right Italian, and when the inquest reopened further doubts emerged. Joseph Burford, another of the lads, told the same story as White and Charles Pickford, but when Thomas Tranter took the stand, his evidence showed obvious differences.

Tranter said that John Pickford had asked Ferrito for the ice cream and not the Italian known as "Steve" whom the others had identified. The man John Pickford spoke to was dark and wore a white slop. The argument started when "Steve" picked up the money and refused to give an ice cream. That man was tall, with light hair, a girl's face and a moustache.

The descriptions of the Italians were becoming confused. "Steve" was tall, light haired and with a moustache, or he was dark haired without a moustache. Ferrito was short, dark and with a moustache; or dark, but no moustache. Which one was it? Also, John Pickford had placed his money on "Steve's" cart, or was it Ferrito's? The only things they did agree over were that the Italians started the fight and one wearing a slop stabbed young Bateman. But who was he?

The only independent witness to come forward was a Mrs Ellen Hart of 1 Jenner Street. She had been walking down Cleveland Road with her husband, Benjamin, when they were passed by a group of Italians running with their carts. The one at the rear stopped, loosed his cart and turned to face the local youths who were chasing them. She saw the Italian strike the leading lad, who then fell onto his back. The Italian then ran off, but Mrs Hart was not sure of the direction that he took.

However, Mrs Hart was quite sure that the lad's assailant wore shirtsleeves and not a slop. She was still there when the policeman arrived with his prisoner but she was not sure that he was the person who attacked Bateman.

At this stage the Coroner thought it best to close the hearing and resume at a much later date when the police might have carried out more detailed investigations.

When the inquest resumed on 21st August the remainder of the local youths gave their evidence. John Dunne and David Costley just reiterated the evidence of previous witnesses. The coroner hoped that John Pickford would clarify what really happened on that evening since his actions seemed to have started the whole affair. As might have been expected, Pickford insisted that the Italians started the violence, even though they had not been provoked. He denied that any of his friends were drunk and no one tried to hit any Italian with a belt. As for the stabbing, he agreed that Ferrito had done it.

Having listened to a series of statements with a decidedly English flavour, the Coroner was convinced that the Italians would produce their own spiced up version of the events. He was to be surpised.

The first Italian called was not a member of the party involved in the fracas. Olimpio Rossi had arrived for the hearing from London, where he lived with his parents at 32 Great Warner Street, Clerkenwell. His evidence was to astound the court.

He told the court that he had known Steven Pacitto (Steve) for three to four years and on the morning of 31st July Pacitto had turned up at his father's grocery shop in London. As usual, they went for a drink at the Queen's Head in Warner Street where Pacitto had told him some disturbing news. He said that he had just come from Wolverhampton because he was in trouble. The evening before he and other Italians had been involved in a fight with a group of English lads.

The lads had started the trouble by demanding ice cream. When they were told that there was none left, one had taken his belt off and beat Pacitto on the back with it. The Italians had run away but were chased. Fearing for his safety because his cart was heavier than the rest and he was at back, he turned to face the youths. When he turned, he drew out his ice pricker. As the first one got to him, Pacitto hit him twice with the pricker. When the lad fell down at his feet, he panicked and ran off. However, what was most curious was that the police had arrested Ferrito for the crime.

Had the police, on the insistence of Charles Pickford, arrested the wrong man? It would seem so, but the Coroner wanted to hear more evidence.

The next witness, Vincenzo Tomasso, also of Warner Street, London, gave his evidence through an interpreter. He confirmed Rossi's story, despite not being an acquaintance of Rossi. He testified that on the evening of Tuesday, 31st July Pacitto arrived at his home during dinner and asked to speak to him. Pacitto repeated the same version of the events in Wolverhampton and asked Tomasso to write to his parents to tell them of his crime.

Pacitto's excuse for not writing himself was that he had little time to do it. What Tomasso did not know was that Pacitto was planning to go to Paris on the advice of another friend. Tomasso told the court that he wrote the following day to Gennaro Pacitto, Steve's brother. A few days later Tomasso received a letter from Steve, which was posted in Paris.

It would seem that the real killer was safe from English justice, but the Coroner was still not thoroughly convinced that Ferrito had nothing to do with the murder. He called James Smith to give evidence, a boy who lived with the Italians at 20 Salop Street.

He had been with the Italians on the night and, although he had not been close enough to hear what passed between the two groups, he had seen Ferrito's cart tip over and the rest of the Italians run past Ferrito, except for Pacitto, who was some 30 to 40 yards behind. Young Smith had helped to pick up Ferrito's cart and as he did, he saw Pacitto rush at one of the Englishmen, who then fell down. Pacitto then ran off and Ferrito followed. Smith thought it strange that the police arrested Ferrito because he had struck no one.

Evidence was mounting in favour of Ferrito. When Joseph Miranda and Samuel Adcock, who had both been involved in the incident, said that they had seen a letter from Steven Pacitto to his brother declaring his guilt, Mr Phillips decided it was in the best interests of justice to adjourn until Gennaro, who was apparently in Britain, could be brought to give evidence.

On 29th August 1888 the hearing resumed with Gennaro Pacitto giving his testimony. He had received two letters from Paris in which his brother admitted the crime, but unfortunately he had burnt both. However, he did have a third letter which he had received on 24th August. In his anger he had torn it up, but fragments remained. Apologising to the court for his lack of understanding of their importance in a trial, he handed over the remnants of the final letter.

> Paris, 23rd August 1888
>
> Dearest Brother,
> I have received yours and understood all that you have said to me, that I cannot come any more in England. That is nothing that I am alone. (TORN) Vincenzo let me run from London, I did not want to run away, but he told me run away, as all the blame will be put on you and Ferrito will be liberated. He wanted me to have my hair dyed. I replied "No", that they might have me arrested (TORN) and now I am turned against.

Clearly the letter was from a very distressed man, but it did not openly admit to the crime. It was a pity that the two previous letters had been destroyed, but the Coroner was now certain that the killer was not in his court. However, there was to be one more twist to the case.

Young James Smith asked to be recalled. He was the only witness to swear that he had actually seen Steven Pacitto stab Bateman, but he pleaded to be allowed to change his statement. Before he did so, the Coroner pointed out that he could be considered an unreliable witness, but Smith wanted to continue.

In his new statement he swore that he had previously been mistaken about the incident. He had come to realise that he had seen Ferrito and Pacitto together as they were being chased, and neither of them had turned to face the English lads. He admitted that he had lied at first because a man called Tomasso Lani had told him what to say. However, Gennaro Pacitto had told him that Lani hated Steven Pacitto and wanted rid of him. Gennaro had persuaded him to tell the truth.

The Coroner had no option but to dismiss all evidence from Smith and instructed the jury to ignore it. That left just one other witness to question – Antonio Ferrito.

When called to the stand it was clear that Ferrito would need help. His highly emotional state and lack of English made him almost unintelligible, and so an interpreter was used. Those two factors turned out to be the major reasons why the police had kept him in custody. Unable to make himself fully understood, he had virtually agreed to their accusations, but in court with an interpreter he could tell his version of the events.

When Ferrito had finished, the Coroner had little difficulty in deciding that the wrong man was in the dock, and so instructed the jury to bring in a verdict of "manslaughter against some person unknown". The jury agreed and Ferrito was released, much to the relief of family and friends. With Steven Pacitto, the possible murderer abroad, the case should have ended there, but there was to be another turn of events.

Towards the end of the year Pacitto returned to England and surrendered to the police, who promptly arrested him for the murder of Bateman. He was taken to Stafford Gaol and his trial started on 30th July 1889, exactly one year on from the fatal stabbing. Once again, the affair was to have startling conclusions.

The jury listened intently as each witness relived their account of the previous year's hearing, each one insisting that what they had testified before was the truth. The local boys were adamant that it was Ferrito who had struck the blow, while the Italians insisted that Steven Pacitto had confessed to the murder.

The only fresh evidence came from Dr Gough, a police surgeon, who had re-examined the body. He said that the wound appeared to have been inflicted by some thin, flat blade such as a knife or stiletto. In his opinion, it could not have been caused by such an instrument as the ice pricker shown to him. So where did that leave Pacitto's confession?

What then were the jury to believe? The Coroner's jury had not indicted Ferrito and the evidence that they had heard would suggest that Pacitto was lying about his involvement in the affair. As Mr Plumtre, defending counsel, so eloquently put it, "they had been called upon to deal with a mystery; that one of these Italians had killed Bateman was certain, but that no one upon responsibility of their oath and conscience was able to say which it was".

In his summing up of the case the judge, Justice Commissioner Philbrick, instructed the jury to bear in mind that it mattered not whether the witnesses were Italian or English; the only question that they had to decide was whether the witnesses were reliable. Clearly one of the Italians had been responsible for the death of Alfred Bateman, but which witnesses could the jury definitely believe? If they had any doubts, then a verdict of "Not Guilty" should be delivered.

The jury returned a verdict of not guilty and Steven Pacitto was discharged.

The Voice of the Dead
(Wolverhampton 1902 – Express & Star)

The starting point of English Criminal Law is that everyone is innocent until proved guilty beyond reasonable doubt. Sometimes this results in an acquittal which, to the layman, seems blatantly foolish, and this certainly happened when Joseph Earp was acquitted of the murder of his wife. The police and the public thought he was guilty, but not the law.

Joseph Earp and his wife, Emma, aged 38, had been married for nineteen years and for most of that time had lived at 3 Philip Street, Wolverhampton. They seemed a happy couple and no evidence was ever given to the contrary. They had seven children, six of them still living at home at the time of the incident. So what happened to cause the tragedy of Wednesday 19th November 1902?

At 10 minutes to 7 on that fateful evening, Joseph Earp had left home, gone straight to Cope's liquor vaults and got deliberately and desperately drunk. He returned home around 11 o'clock barely able to stand, and an argument broke out with his wife. That was when Emma Earp was set alight, accidentally or deliberately, by a paraffin lamp which smashed against her back.

Realising that she was on fire, Emma ran out into the street screaming for help to douse the flames. So fierce was the blaze and so wild her panic that it took a long time to calm her down and put out the fire. When Constable Cooper arrived he removed the remainder of her smouldering garments and took her to Wolverhampton General Hospital.

Before being taken to the hospital though, Emma Earp had told Detective Sergeant Vincent what had happened in her home and he had gone there to question Joseph. He found Joseph Earp very drunk and quite incapable of remembering anything that had happened. Getting no help, Vincent decided to arrest Earp for attempted murder and took him to the police station.

The charge of attempted murder was to change dramatically on the morning of 22nd November when Emma Earp died. She never regained consciousness sufficiently to be interviewed by the police for a written statement. All that they had was the garbled account heard by Sergeant Vincent on the night of the incident.

THE WOLVERHAMPTON LAMP-THROWING CASE.

DEATH OF MRS EARP.

HUSBAND CHARGED WITH MURDER.

REMAND UNTIL THURSDAY.

When the Coroner opened the inquest on the afternoon of Tuesday 22nd November one thing soon became clear. There were many witnesses to describe what had happened outside the Earp's house, but the only people who knew what had happened inside were Joseph and his wife.

The Coroner knew that he had a difficult case on his hands. Most of those present were convinced that Joseph Earp had killed his wife, but what would the law say the Coroner must do? Hoping some evidence might emerge that would ease his decision by making the facts clear, he allowed the hearing to go ahead.

Winifred Shale lived at 23 Baker Street which backed on to Philip Street. She told the court that on the evening of 19th November she had been in her kitchen at about 11 o'clock when she heard a woman screaming "Murder!"

117

at least four times. Before that she had heard a noise like falling and breaking glass. She had opened her front door to see Emma Earp standing at the corner of Philip Street enveloped in flames from head to waist.

Pulling off her apron, Mrs Shale had dashed to the woman to douse the flames and other people arrived on the scene. However, the poor woman was in such agony that she did not allow anyone to touch her, but ran off into Dale Street, still on fire. It was there that a man named Lester forced Mrs Earp to the ground and rolled her over and over to put out the fire. That was when Constable Cooper had arrived and removed the woman's clothing.

Mary Wright of 1 Philip Street said that after all the commotion had finished, she and a Mrs Baugh had gone into the Earp's kitchen to find out whether the children were safe. There had been no light in the room except from the fire grate. Joseph Earp, plainly drunk, was sitting by the fire. When the two women asked him where his wife was, all that he said was that he didn't know and that he hadn't seen her.

Both women noticed the remains of a broken glass lamp on the kitchen table and when they asked Earp why it was broken, he again replied that he didn't know. Realising that they had little chance of getting any sense out of the man, they had gone upstairs to look for the children. Assuring themselves that they were safe, they had left the house.

Another woman named Mitchell testified that she had heard glass breaking on the fatal night and then saw Mrs Earp in flames in the street, screaming aloud. Later she had witnessed Joseph Earp kicking the burner from a lamp and some broken glass out of his house into the street. He had also kicked out a piece of carpet that was still on fire. After that Earp had fetched a child's frock that he threw onto the flames to douse them. That done, he returned to the house and closed the door.

Constable Cooper said that on the evening of 19th November at just after 11 o'clock, he had been on duty in Merridale Street when he heard screams coming from Dale Street. Running to the scene, he found Mrs Earp sitting on the ground still burning. Wrapping his cape around the woman, he had managed to extinguish the last of the fire and remove her smouldering clothing. At that point Sergeant Vincent arrived and spoke to the woman, then told Cooper to take Emma Earp to the hospital. Returning to the scene later, he had collected several pieces of burnt clothing for evidence.

Sergeant Vincent told the court that when he had arrived in Dale Street, Mrs Earp had been seated on a chair outside number 45 wrapped in the constable's cape. He offered to treat her burns but the woman had preferred to go to hospital. Before the constable took her there Vincent asked her what had happened.

Emma Earp told him that her husband had arrived home at about 10 minutes to 11 and was very drunk. He sat down by the fire but had scarcely been seated when he had started to grumble to himself. Then he took off his coat and threw it at her. Suddenly and without warning, he picked up the paraffin lamp and hurled it at her. It had struck her on the body and smashed, spilling oil all over her. The oil had immediately caught fire and in her panic, she had run out in to the street where a man had put out the flames.

Sergeant Vincent went on to tell the court that after he had sent Mrs Earp to hospital with Constable Cooper, he went to the Earp's house to question the husband. Joseph Earp was indeed very drunk. The detective noticed some broken glass on the floor and a strong smell of paraffin. Outside the door he found burning rubbish that included the remains of a burner from a lamp.

Getting no replies to any of his questions from Joseph Earp, he decided to take him to the police station. The following morning he charged him with inflicting grievous bodily harm on Mrs Earp, and when the woman died he had changed that charge to one of murder.

Sergeant Vincent was at pains to make the court understand that Earp showed no remorse. Each time the prisoner was questioned he refused to make any comment and remained stubbornly silent. In fact, the only person to whom Earp spoke was his brother, William.

William's evidence was brief. When he told Joseph that he had been charged with throwing something at his wife and she was nearly dead, all that Joseph had said was, "I have not done anything, Bill". However, William had to admit that Joseph had been drunk.

With no witness having anything to say which might help Joseph Earp, and all the evidence suggesting his guilt, everyone present seemed convinced that the case was cut and dried. Joseph Earp must be guilty of murdering his wife. The Coroner surprised them.

Summing up, Coroner Willcock said that there had been only Joseph and his wife present in the living room at the time of the incident. Undoubtedly, Mrs

Earp had died from massive burns, but as to who had inflicted them, there was some doubt. There was no evidence from within the house that the lamp had in fact been thrown. It might have been knocked off the table accidentally, even by Mrs Earp herself.

The only evidence of what had happened in the room was what Emma Earp had said to the police, but since she had died, her words were being reported by another person, and therefore hearsay. In such cases juries can't judge the demeanour of the witness and they can't be cross examined. There were in the Victorian era then and there still are, quite strict rules about admitting the statements of dead people as evidence.

Explaining to the jury the law as it was in 1902, Coroner Willcock said he was bound to tell them that "conversations were not evidence of the facts therein disclosed, but were only evidence that a complaint had been made". He went on to say that the statement made by Mrs Earp to Sergeant Vincent was not admissible because it was made in the absence of her husband, the only other witness to what actually took place at number 3 Philip Street that night. Had the statement been taken under the correct procedure, then it would have certainly been admissible.

As there was no other evidence, Willcock left it to the jury to decide Joseph Earp's fate. Having carefully studied the coroner's advice, they returned a verdict of "Death from burns and shock", but declared that there was not sufficient evidence to show how the injuries were caused.

The Coroner's jury did not indict Earp, but there was a different sentiment in the Magistrates' Court. On application by the police they decided that Earp had a case to answer and he was remanded to the Assizes at Stafford, where they hoped that Mrs Earp's statement might be admissible as evidence.

The trial opened on 6th December 1902 with Commissioner John Forbes as judge. Mr Hill, for the Prosecution, explained to the jury that Joseph Earp had been committed for trial by the Magistrates and not the Coroner's jury, who had returned an open verdict at the inquest. Having briefly explained the circumstances by which Emma Earp had lost her life, Hill then wanted to tell the jury of Emma's conversation with Sergeant Vincent. Before he could begin the judge pointed out that her statement was not admissible as evidence.

Fully prepared for this, Mr Hill cited some legal precedents, or similar cases, in which such evidence had been permitted. In *Rex versus Foster* in 1834 just such a statement had been allowed because it had been made "as soon after the occurrence of the crime as could be reasonably expected". Surely Mrs Earp's statement was similar?

The judge updated Mr Hill's law, citing a more recent case where similar evidence had not been allowed. He pointed out that Emma Earp's statement had not been made immediately after the event and the accused, the only other witness to the tragedy, had not been present when she had made her statement. Under those circumstances he had no other option but to refuse the evidence, but he would permit the case to continue.

Having produced the same witnesses who appeared at the inquest, Mr Hill then cross examined Joseph Earp, hoping to throw some new light on the events of 19th November. It soon became clear that he had been so drunk that he had little recollection of anything that had happened, or did not want to remember.

The judge saw that no new evidence was forthcoming and advised both counsel to prepare their final submissions.

Hill was certain the Defence would claim that the terrible incident had been nothing more than a sad accident and he aimed to discredit that theory. Would the poor woman, he asked the jury, have cried "Murder", if she had merely been set alight accidentally? Surely not. And the prisoner? No matter how drunk he had been, surely he would have tried to do something about the flames. He did nothing.

If it had been an accident, would the woman have dashed into the street for help? Surely she would expect her husband to help, but what did he do – nothing! Even the police had asked him, "Where is your wife?", to which he had simply replied, "Find her". Those, Mr Hill argued, were the words and actions of a callous man, deep in violent passion. As to the actual burns, the fact that most of them had been on the woman's back surely indicated that she had tried to avoid the lamp that had been deliberately thrown at her.

For the Defence, Mr Plumtre pointed out that none of the Earp's neighbours had heard an argument before the fire. If Joseph Earp had been in such a drunken frenzy, then surely they would have heard something? The accused, Mr Plumtre admitted, had been very drunk, but he had still tried to extinguish the fire in his house, which proved that he had been trying to preserve his home and not wreck it. If Emma Earp had stayed inside, he would have tried to help her also.

As to the cries of "Murder", would not anyone on fire simply mean that the flames were killing them? She did not mean that her husband had tried to kill her, but that she was dying from catching fire – catching fire because of an accidental explosion of the lamp, a daily event with cheap lamps.

In his final plea to the jury Plumtre had to admit that "It was a case merged in darkness; there was no light to show how the occurrence had happened"; but he felt sure that "in this country, men's lives were not taken away on probabilities".

It did not take the jury long to find Earp not guilty, but many people were left with the feeling that he had been acquitted on a legal technicality.

Murder

" … she did not come home on that Saturday night, and at about 6 o'clock the following evening her body was found outside a shed in the tennis club grounds."

"… the sexton was making his way to the church along the Avon's bank when his eye was caught by a gleam in the grass. Stooping, he found a pair of gold rimmed spectacles."

"They noticed a dark shape huddled in the trench by the old shaft but they ignore it, believing to be a drunk sleeping off his beer."

"… when the coffin was opened Thomas, who had been buried face upwards, was lying face down…"

"There is nothing which takes fingerprints as well as glass. On Mr Newton's milk bottle the burglar and killer had left his signature, which Scotland Yard soon identified as that of a West Bromwich man …"

Barrie Roberts's two collections of murders draw on cases from 1760 to the 1960s committed in all corners of the Midlands. Meet the boy who stole bones from a graveyard, the detective who didn't see a murderer board the train, the housekeeper daed in a locked room, the lodger who fell for his landlady and the rich brewer who didn't kill his lover. Some murders were never solved but one killer was caught by chance after 25 years. Greed, and jelousy, guns, knives and poison all appear in these absorbing pages.

Midland
Murders & Mysteries
(ISBN 1-898136-14-9)

Murder
in the Midlands
(ISBN 1-898136-19-X)

John Roberts

Quercus

£7.95 each, post free in UK
67 Cliffe Way, Warwick CV34 5JG
Tel/fax 01926776363
Email: john@walkwaysquercus.fsbusiness.co.uk